"This read is pure joy. It has encouraged me to take the first of many walks on the wild side of life."

—From Wilted to Wild

"*Born to Be Wild* will take you on a wild ride down memory lane and put fun back into your everyday life."

—Born to Be Wild and Didn't Know It

"This book shows you how to live and laugh, play and find joy amid the stuff in your life, and allow yourself to be a little '*un*-responsible' every now and then."

—Learning to Enjoy the Process

"I can't wait to give a copy of this book to all of my middle-aged, menopausal, soul-searching friends."

—Harley Mama

"Reading this book made me want to give God a round of applause for the craziness of life!"

—Crazy Nana

"I love a read that makes you laugh out loud. This girl's antics keep you wanting more and show you that growing old and having fun doing it have God's complete approval."

—White Water Canoeing Mama

"Any book that can relate turkey giblets to the Scripture should be a best-seller!"

—Ex–Party Pooper

"What a hoot! This book is so funny! There were times I had to put it down just to relax my face."

—Moo the Clown

BORN TO BE WILD

REDISCOVER
THE FREEDOM
OF FUN

JILL BAUGHAN

NEW HOPE
PUBLISHERS

BIRMINGHAM, ALABAMA

New Hope® Publishers
P. O. Box 12065
Birmingham, AL 35202-2065
www.newhopepublishers.com

Library of Congress Cataloging-in-Publication Data

Baughan, Jill.
  Born to be wild : rediscover the freedom of fun / Jill Baughan.
    p. cm.
  Includes bibliographical references.
  ISBN 1-59669-048-8 (soft cover)
   1. Christian women—Religious life. I. Title.
  BV4527.B38 2006
  248.8'43—dc22
          2006012448

ISBN-10: 1-59669-048-8
ISBN-13: 978-1-59669-048-6

N074131 • 0906 • 5.5M1

WITH PRAYERS FOR

THE WILDEST OF

JOURNEYS THROUGH LIFE,

I DEDICATE THIS BOOK TO YOU,
MY NEW BEST FRIEND.

Get your motor runnin...

TABLE OF
CONTENTS

STORIES FROM ALL *Seasons of Life*

CHILDHOOD

TABLE OF CONTENTS

TABLE OF CONTENTS

MIDDLE ADULTHOOD

THE REST OF LIFE

On the outside chance that anyone actually reads "Acknowledgments," I'd like you to know that there are more than a few people who are really responsible for making this book happen. I am forever indebted to...

Everyone who read the proposal and so generously and enthusiastically gave me feedback: Thank you, my friends, for being the wildest of the wild!

Everyone who let me use their story: I *really* hope I asked your permission first, and if I didn't, I thank you for being okay with me exposing a few details of your private life to the public at large.

Andrea Mullins, Rebecca England, Tina Atchenson, Wendy Wakefield, Jean Baswell, and anyone else from New Hope who laid a helping hand on this manuscript: Thank you so much for believing that this message was worth sharing! We must get together for a motorcycle ride some day...

Val Jackson: We've been friends since we were two, and we've shared a lot of "firsts." Thanks for being with me on my very first Tilt-A-Whirl adventure. May the thrill rides never end. Hee rah and yee hah!

Janet Quiroga, college buddy and lifelong friend: Thanks for teaching me the meaning of "Let's howl!" We must never, *ever* stop!

Beth Saunders: Thanks for being a sounding board during countless walks and talks. You don't have to read this book; you've heard it all already—mostly during intense "training" sessions. Riiight?

Sandy Weakley (aka Moo the Clown): From impersonating Elvis to dressing up like a Ping-Pong ball, you've shown me that life can be one crazy costume change after another. Thanks for many years of fun with goofy getups!

ACKNOWLEDGMENTS

ACKNOWLEDGMENTS

Sue Rye, Harley Mama: I've never had so much fun watching someone have fun! Thanks for not fainting when "Mr. Steppenwolf" showed up at the door.

John Smorto, the Ultimate Harley Guy: You did good! Ride on...

Doug Grote: Thanks for calling me up a few strategic Monday mornings and saying, "I'm waitin', Baughan." Without your most sensitive admonitions to turn in my week's writing, it'd probably be another 16 years before I finished this book.

Nancy Sprinkle: I can never thank you enough for praying for me—even through the *years* I spent telling people, "Oh yes, I'm writing a book...should be done any minute now!"

Curtis and Bea Shepperson of Windy Hill Farm: You made my dream come true by being willing to bring your sweet little Sierra into my home. Tarzan couldn't have done it better!

Arlene and Arthur Baughan: Thanks for treating me like your own all these many years and letting me share your oh-so-unique relationship with the rest of the world.

My sister-in-law, Marge Ellis: Thanks for being my wonderful friend. Could two spirits be any more kindred? I think not! Here's to many more "Thelma and Louise" road trips!

My mom, Mary Ellis: In addition to thanking you for giving me life, I must thank you for giving me one of the finest moments of my life: you, me, and the ape, together on film for all posterity to gaze upon in wonder.

My daddy, Curtis Ellis: Thanks for the picture you gave me of the Heavenly Father. See you later.

My brother, Ted Ellis, the honorable mayor of Bluffton, Indiana: These stories from my childhood are waayyy too familiar to you. Thanks for teaching me a lot of things that seem goofy to a lot of people but are priceless to me.

The family portrait participants (Andy, Nikki, Trey, Curtis, Becky, Ted, Marge, Keith, Jamie, Ben, and Mom): Thanks for being such good sports about gathering for the photo op of a lifetime. Here's to a gene pool like no other...

Grandmas Pinney and Ellis: Thank you for actually believing that your grandchildren were perfect. I can still feel it.

My daughter and son-in-law, Jamie and Keith Rodden: Thanks for being willing to share your wedding festivities with a chimpanzee. Someday you'll look back and actually thank me for it...honest.

My husband, Ben: Oh my, the thank-yous to you will never end. Thanks for desperately begging me (you were on your hands *and* knees, as I recall) to marry you; thanks for being a steady source of joy in the ups and downs of our life together; and thanks for putting me first on your list. I love you, too.

And finally, to...

Foreign Young Man: I don't really want to incriminate you by using your name, but if you're reading this, you know who you are. Thanks for giving me a chance to wear a great dress.

ACKNOWLEDGMENTS

I t took me 16 years to write this book. I'm not sure why. Maybe because my life has been filled with distractions and interruptions: like Christmas…and my daughter's graduation from elementary school…and middle school…and high school…and college. And then there was grocery shopping and the laundry and, of course, lunch.

I am easily distracted.

Also, I cannot stand to pass up an opportunity to goof off. Something fun comes along, and I think: "The work will always be there. The fun? Maybe not." I can't even dust the piano without sitting down to make some music first, so of course I have spent much of the past 16 years playing around and, unfortunately, simultaneously living in guilt, wondering why I've always had so much trouble buckling down and keeping my nose to the grindstone.

I guess, then, it should be no surprise to anyone that, for many years, I had to be dragged kicking and screaming from one stage of life to the next, ever dreading the Land of Responsible Adulthood looming before me, fearing that every step closer to growing up was also a step closer to the end of the good life. I wasn't what you'd call irresponsible—just a "fun junkie" with an inordinate need to be entertained. And I thought it was a vice…a curse of some sort, like the eighth deadly sin. But I have learned otherwise.

"Oh, crazy girl," I now say to myself, "it's not a curse at all, but a gift."

You see, I believe that we begin our existence with an unlimited capacity for fun. Then life starts to happen: we are distracted from our playtime because people are always urging us to exercise self-discipline. There's a lot of work to do, you know.

And then after we've lived and worked a while, we get our first taste of soul sadness. We lose something—our innocence or a dream falls by the wayside—or we lose

INTRODUCTION

someone very dear through relocation or death or desertion. We start growing up and accumulating a lot of responsibility, like jobs and relationships and mortgages on houses that we have to clean. In the midst of it all, we realize one day it's been a while since we had some rollicking fun. And we've almost forgotten how to have the kind of fun that was so easy to have when life was a lot simpler, before we lost and found so much.

Maybe you're at an age at which you find yourself doing a fair amount of reflecting on your life—looking back at your past, taking stock of your present, and wondering about your future. Maybe you are enjoying the journey most of the time. Then again, maybe you are standing at this odd kind of crossroads with a fair amount of dismay or confusion or fear or, most of all, longing: longing for more—more time (both in a day and on this earth), more energy, more passion, more adventure.

I understand.

A long time ago, I used to think that women at the middle stage of life were ready to rein it in. Now I know the truth: we just want to bust out. Underneath all that life junk is a spirit that wants to, as Wilbur the Pig said in Charlotte's Web, "run and jump and make merry." If only we could find the time...or the reason...or the heart.

Oh, crazy girl. If you know God, you already have all three. It's just a matter of taking the time He's given you...of being present to every occasion that calls for celebration...of resurrecting that joy that maybe is so deep in your heart you haven't seen it for a long time. But it's there, I promise, waiting to be brought back to life. It's there, just begging the untamed woman inside you to come out and play—the very woman who (in my mind) was the inspiration for Steppenwolf's song of the '60s, "Born to Be Wild."

Surely you are familiar with this wide-open invitation to freedom and adventure, and surely you know it sounds best at a decibel level that actually frightens the tweeters and woofers of your sound system. Personally, I love to crank that baby up and imagine myself on a motorcycle, wind in my face and bugs in my teeth, heading off under a bright blue sky on an endless road of possibilities.

Great song. Great feeling.

I am convinced that it's my song...and yours, too.

Oh, you may not describe yourself as wild—especially if it brings to mind a lot of "heavy metal thunder." But consider this: one of the definitions in my dictionary for wild is "passionately eager or enthusiastic." Now that has a nice ring to it. And sometime soon when you find yourself wistfully surveying your days, when your heart travels over the innocence and trauma of your childhood, heads through your cheerleading/dorky/care-free/tortured adolescence, and moves on to your introduction to adulthood only to land smack-dab in the middle of your so-called life, I want you to remember my own great revelation—the one that has taken me a mere 16 years to realize. That is this: even when part of me mourns what is lost, sighs at what's here, and trembles a little at what's to come, I still want to run out and toilet paper somebody's house; I still want to swing like Tarzan from a vine; the very heart of me still wants to hop onto my "inner Harley" and ride off in a cloud of bliss because...really... I know that, in the best and the worst of times, God created me to be passionately eager and enthusiastic.

I really was born to be wild. And so, I am certain, were you.

STORIES FROM

CHILDHOOD

BIG DUMB FUN

1

DO IT
THE WAY YOU
USED TO.

There's nothing like revisiting some "big dumb fun" of childhood to teach you a lesson or two about God's gift of play.

My opportunity came a couple years ago when I met my childhood friend Val Jackson in uptown Bluffton, Indiana, for a week of immature behavior at the annual Bluffton Street Fair. The fair has been a tradition in my hometown for about a hundred years. Main and Market Streets are blocked off for a week to make way for a hoo-ha of rides and games (Whack-a-Chicken and the Mouse Game were my favorites) and parades of varying themes. I have great memories of the day we would be released from school early, and all school children would march in a parade. Looking back, I have to wonder *why* in the world people found this so fascinating, but it generated even more excitement than the farm implement parade— a grand succession of tractors, plows, combines, and manure spreaders. (I think you have to be from the Midwest to work up some enthusiasm for that one.) Anyway, I remember being put in a row with about seven or eight other kids; our teachers then gave us a long wooden rod to hold on to—either to keep us in a straight line or to keep us from wandering off when we passed the pony rides. Then we just marched—up Main Street and down Market Street, waving at people on the sidelines who were cheering at us like we were Neil Armstrong just back from the moon. It was indescribable fun, feeling like celebrities, being out of school, and looking forward to eating the most exquisite junk food on earth and then hurling it around on a few rides.

Which brings me to my week of ultimate reminiscent play.

The week I went back to the street fair as an adult, Val and I met up and had contests to see how many fried things we could eat in a row—four! And so much to choose from: corn dogs, funnel cakes, elephant ears, fried potatoes, blooming onions, fried green tomatoes, onion rings, fried pork rinds, and one of my favorites, the giant fried tenderloin—a hunk o' pork about the size of your average Frisbee.

Then we decided to try a couple of rides we hadn't been on since we were about 12. Our first choice was the Scrambler. We thought this was a safe one to ride after eating four fried things, because it doesn't leave the ground, take deep plunges, or flip you upside down. We did not take into account the fact that it goes around in circles and violently heaves you to and fro. We also did not take into account that the guy running the ride thought we were cute and decided to put it in overdrive for an extra long time. It was fun at first, getting tossed all over each other, hurtled about…but after a while, it was obvious that this thing runs much faster nowadays (really, I mean it) than it did when I was 12. We started to feel reeeeally bad, but we were having such a good time in spite of it. Never before in my life had I wanted to laugh and throw up simultaneously—an odd sensation.

Anyway, when the Scrambler finally stopped, we staggered out of the car, thoroughly scrambled, and decided that what we needed to make us feel better was some ice cream. Yes, indeedy. So we ate ice cream. Then we went on another childhood favorite, the Tilt-A-Whirl. Do I need to tell you that after four fried things and a few scoops of ice cream, this one just about did me in? Still, I knew I would do it all over again if I had the chance; I just couldn't get enough. When the week was over, I had a cholesterol hangover and a permanent case of vertigo, but I couldn't wait for another go at it next year.

What made it such a memorable experience? I mean, this fair is not Disney World or even Six Flags Over Whatever, but I was able to enter into the joy I experienced as a kid and, for a while, tap into a feeling of freedom, and abandon all the common sense that we lug around as the baggage of adulthood.

Often we think of childhood activities as just that—fun stuff that you could only do as a kid, but not any more. And, okay, there *are* a few things that you might not be able to do now that you did when you were six. For instance, I can't find anyone brave enough to heave me onto their shoulders so I can see the parade above the crowd at the street fair. And while it's true that a *revisit* certainly won't be just like it was when you were a kid, it can revive the playful spirit inside you that's been waiting to come out. You can experience some reminiscent play with an added dimension—freedom and fun woven into the tapestry of the rest of your days.

You may be in serious need of some relief from your serious life right now; you may be longing for some excitement or some stimulating change; or maybe you've been dealing with a lot of change that's far from stimulating, and you just want to be able to count on the stability of a few things. Maybe you need a break.

In 2 Corinthians 5:17, Paul gives us great hope for such a break in his reminder to the Corinthians that *"if anyone is in Christ, he is a new creation; the old has gone, the new has come!"*—not only in the form of a new life in Him, but also as a new perspective on your old life.

And, trust me, if you take the time to revisit the heart of your childhood, you will certainly come away with a thankful—and maybe lighter—heart as a gift from God who makes all things new.

TRY THIS

Take out a piece of paper and brainstorm for 15 minutes about activities you used to love. Go as far back in your life as you can, and don't censor yourself! No item in a brainstorm is too outrageous. Then take a good long look at the list, and brainstorm some ideas about ways you could revisit as many of those activities as possible.

SWEAT IT OUT

2

TAKE THE GIFT OF A SECOND CHANCE.

If you've ever been granted a second chance to do something fun when you so stupidly passed up your first chance, you know the definition of gratitude. It's a concept I'm very familiar with, since I started making stupid decisions at a young age. One of them was life changing.

When I was about six years old, my mom came into my room one day with a proposition: "How," she asked, "would you like to take tap dancing lessons?" Instantly, I had a vision: frilly tutus, rouged cheeks, shiny shoes that made cool noise, and best of all, the chance to get up on a stage and show it all off for an audience. Just as quickly, though, came another, more ominous vision: being forced to spend hours hoofing it in a sweaty dance studio when I'd rather be, say, watching TV and finding new hiding places for contraband sucker sticks. Hmmm.... A decision of this magnitude, I knew, called for a consultation with my two imaginary friends, Toady and Joan Myers. I had invented these buddies in my mind to conjure up when I needed a couple of playmates or some strategic advice. Toady, as I recall, was egg shaped and wore little shorts on his stick-shaped legs. He looked a lot like Humpty Dumpty. Joan Myers looked like the farmer's wife from "The Farmer in the Dell"—an elderly woman with a printed scarf on her head. Where in the *world* I dug up these names and images I have no idea; I only know that the three of us were very close— so close that my brother, Ted, and his friends knew that the one way to make me cry was to tell me they were going to force Joan Myers into the kitchen one day and make her crack Toady over a frying pan and scramble him into oblivion.

Anyway, I quickly asked their opinion of the situation, and they told me to ask Mom a question—one that would alter the course of my life: "Would I have to practice?"

"Well, of course," she said, looking at me curiously.

I mentally weighed the options in my six-year-old mind: tutu on one hand, sweating on the other; tutu, sweat; tutu, sweat. Finally, I decided I could go *buy* a tutu and sit around in it at home without sweating.

"No thanks," I told her, resolutely. And that was that...until....

I had a chance to go to a dance recital to watch a friend perform. I had never seen such a dazzling array of pink tulle and sequins in my life, not to mention the spectacle of what looked like to me hundreds of little girls my age with makeup on their faces and hair lacquered to their heads to get it to stay in a little knot on top—all shuffling off to Buffalo in a fascinating kind of synchronized stampede.

I was overcome with remorse, knowing that I had blown any chance of ever being part of that magic because, after all, I was seven and too old, I thought, to learn to dance.

One more opportunity came in the form of my mother, a year later, bearing yet another proposition: "How," she asked, "would you like to take piano lessons?" Instantly, I had a vision: I was at the piano, my fingers whizzing up and down the keyboard, astounding my audience with original renditions of "Froggie Went A-Courtin'," "Hound Dog," and selections from the latest collection of Alvin and the Chipmunks. Just as quickly, though, came another, more ominous vision: being forced to spend hours on a piano bench, sweating it out (Is there a phobia name for "fear of perspiration"?), laboring over song after song, when I'd rather be, say, dancing around the house in a tutu. I was torn, but I remembered the advice from my invisible duo the last time I was faced with this decision…so I asked the other question that would alter my life.

"Would I have to practice?"

"Well, of course," she said, looking at me this time with more exasperation than curiosity.

I mentally weighed the options in my seven-year-old mind: astounding my audience on one hand, sweating on the other; astounding, sweating; astounding, sweating. Finally, I decided that I could probably teach myself to play the piano. But just as I was about to say, "No thanks," yet again, I remembered my opportunity lost. I remembered how awful it felt to wish I had said yes to tap dancing. I remembered my longing for lacquered hair. I didn't want to feel that way again, ever.

So I said, "Yes."

And it really did change my life.

No, I didn't become a concert pianist; I didn't even major in music in college.

But playing the piano taught me so much—about humility, for instance. My first recital was six months after I started taking lessons. I was to play "Forest Dawn," and since I had found that I adored playing and had become obsessive about practicing, I had the song nailed.

I was one of the youngest and newest, so I was one of the first on the roster. When Mrs. Pease announced my name, I proudly went up to the bench, sat down…and freaked. All of a sudden, I became acutely aware of the millions of people who were sitting silently behind me, waiting for me to do something. My mind froze. My hands froze. But although I was only seven, I was pretty good at "solitary conversation" (having practiced on Toady and Joan Myers), so I talked myself into relative calm.

My hands finally found the keys, and my mind thawed out enough to begin the song. And in moments, I was sailing along, so glad to be in the groove…until I ran out of keys.

Apparently, I had started up a couple octaves too high, and at that particular height, there was an insufficient number of ivories to finish the song as written.

My mind froze. My hands froze. And once again, I became acutely aware of the millions of people who were sitting silently behind me, waiting for me to do something. Anything. Only this time I had the added bonus of knowing I had screwed up. In fact, I was in the process of screwing up at that very moment. It was awful.

But after what seemed like 30 minutes of sitting there with my parents and grandmas and friends and God waiting for me to get it together, I did. I started over, played the thing, and couldn't get to my seat fast enough.

Despite my family's reassurance that I had made a great recovery, I cried all the way home. But I learned one thing that day: no matter how good you think you are, you're never infallible, you've never really got it all together, and just when your head gets about this big, you may find yourself dialing a 911 to your imaginary friends.

Even so, I continued to enjoy playing piano into adolescence; it gave me enormous confidence in, of all things, my physical strength.

I was part of a stage band in high school, and we always had great fun playing at dinners and such. One particular evening at a dinner, we were setting up our instruments, and I had to play the only keyboard they had: a large upright piano. It had to be moved, so despite the sign that said "Do not move this piano," (I just figured they didn't want it stolen), I tried to push it a little. It didn't budge. I pushed it again. No luck. "Wow," I thought, "this is one heavy instrument"; then I gave it a big ol' shove.

Bad move. The upright became a downright with a big crash, hitting the wall and somebody's trombone on the way to the floor. I'll never forget what it felt like to have everyone stop eating and turn to look at the girl lying on the fallen piano. Our band leader later told me that the manager of the building said that "some gorilla must have knocked that thing over," so they gave me the nickname "Godzilla," which of course really helped my body confidence during the rest of high school.

Playing the piano broadened my world, as I accompanied singing groups and went on trips in college; it has been my privilege to be a part of two most significant days in people's lives: their weddings and their funerals; and best of all, it has introduced me to church families, and given me the honor of being part of worship teams whose complete delight is to help people encounter God.

So it's no big deal that I never learned to tap dance. I could do that now if I wanted to! It *is* a big deal that, even if you miss an opportunity the first time around, you can count on God to keep offering up joy on a regular basis.

Because of this, I take a lot of comfort in reading Lamentations 3:22–23. Even though this is a book of mourning, consumed with Jeremiah's predictions of the destruction of Jerusalem, he reminds us that even in sorrow, even in pain, even in the middle of our own stupid decisions, that God's *"compassions never fail. They are new every morning; great is* [His] *faithfulness."*

And God Himself reminds me of this early every morning when I come and sit at this desk in the dark. No matter what the season—even if it's freezing cold and the heat is on inside, or it's steamy hot and the air conditioning is running—I crack the window just so I can listen to the world wake up in the woods behind our house.

It never fails: the night sounds of crickets, cicadas, owls, and unidentified rustlings in the woods slowly—with only a song or two at first—give way to morning sounds of birds singing. Daylight always comes; thousands and thousands of times in my life and yours, the sun rises with God in it, saying, like a personal trainer, "Okay, fresh day! Try it again...and yes, you'll have to practice!"

And morning after morning, I thank Him for another second chance to do just that.

TRY THIS

Have you been offered a second chance at some fun you missed—maybe yesterday, maybe long ago? Make good use of that second chance now!

WHO ARE YOU?

3

W ho were you in school? The geek? The nerd? The popular one? The quiet one? The sporty one? I personally was defined by other people as the big one.

It all started in kindergarten. I was born on October 2, and the deadline for starting school was October 1; my mother decided (wisely, in my case) to wait for another year to send me to school. Consequently, she reasoned, I would be more mature and able to handle academic and social pressures so consuming during the K years. I would also be bigger, since I was almost a year older than almost everybody in the class.

This may not be a challenge for a boy, since boys put a lot of stock in bigness, but for a girl to tower over the rest of the class...

DESCRIBE YOURSELF IN A DIFFERENT WAY.

well, it just feels weird, that's all. Weird enough that one little guy saw fit to nickname me Big Truck. He loved using this name to summon my attention at different times, as in "Hey, Big Truck, pass the crayons." Or "Hey, Big Truck, what's for lunch?" Fortunately, he was too young to be familiar with the classics like "How's the weather up there?" Still, it hurt my feelings beyond words, made me self-conscious about my towering height, and was my first taste of how much power other people could have over my self-image if I let them. For some odd reason, it never occurred to me to counter his attack with a "Hey, Pasty-Faced Shrimp."

The second major encounter involving my size happened on the playground in the third grade during a kickball game. I was not the greatest athlete, but everybody had to play that day for some reason. So another little guy (we'll call him Butch) was pitching the ball to me. He rolled it, and I ran to nail the thing with all my might, aiming my foot for a vicious attack. Well, give me an A for effort. I flung my leg in the direction of the ball and completely missed it, which was bad enough. But worse than that, just at that moment, a good stiff wind caught my dress and blew it straight up into my face. And Butch had a heyday, yelling, "Hey, Big Panties! You missed!"

Really, as I write this, it's almost funny. In fact, my husband has actually *laughed* at this story...but at the time, I was absolutely mortified. I remember wanting to knock the kid into next week, but the wind was still blowing, and I was afraid of ballooning into another side show, so I told myself I didn't care. Didn't care? I still remember it more than 40 years later.

In only a couple of years, it happened again. This time, I was with my older brother, who was a senior in high school, staying after school working on the student newspaper. He introduced me to the faculty sponsor, Mr. Klutz, by telling him that I was his little sister in the fifth grade. And I will never forget Mr. Klutz's response: "*Fifth grade*?" he said, with his eyes popping. "She's bigger than my *wife*!"

Big Truck, Big Panties, *bigger* than my wife. Do we see a pattern emerging here?

And to be honest, I was not getting any smaller. I was the secretary of our eighth grade class; in the yearbook picture of the president, the vice president (both boys), and me, I dwarf them, almost as if someone superimposed one of their mothers next to them.

Eventually, most people caught up to my size, but I remained forever in my mind defined as "big."

You, too, may have grown up describing yourself in a way that really doesn't describe you at all: by your size, your hair, your parents, your money (or lack of it), or any one of a number of labels people imposed on you...or you imposed on yourself.

Maybe, at this time of life, you are struggling with an odd kind of identity crisis, as family dynamics change, and your own longings start to surface. "Who am I," you might ask, "now that _____" (my children are grown and don't need me so much, I'm burned out on this job I've been doing for years, I'm realizing I don't have an unlimited amount of time on this earth to fulfill my dreams).

First of all, remember that our true identity comes from God—the One who made us, the One who knows us better than we know ourselves. And it's so reassuring to be able to say to God, as David did in Psalm 139:

> Oh LORD, *you have searched me*
> *and you know me.*
> You know when I sit and when I rise;
> *you perceive my thoughts from afar.*
> You discern my going out and my lying down;
> *you are familiar with all my ways*
> Before a word is on my tongue,
> *you know it completely, O* LORD.

—Psalm 139:1–4

For you created my inmost being;
        you knit me together in my mother's womb.
—Psalm 139:13

All the days ordained for me
        were written in your book
        before one of them came to be.
—Psalm 139:16

Search me, O God, and know my heart.
—Psalm 139:23

Or maybe you find your reassurance in a personalized version, like mine:

Lord, You know my every move.
You know every time I am struck with envy
        and sadness or emptiness.
You know every place I go:
        to the gym, to the mall, to the fridge.
You know my tendency to use food for comfort,
        my every mood swing, every dark thought,
        every crazy idea, every longing.
You know all the things I want to say and don't,
        and all the things I do say and shouldn't.
You created my body, yes, every "big" bone of it.
Help me to appreciate the body you have given me
        and to find freedom in it.
How will I make the most of these days?
I hate the thought of looking back over my life
        and regretting the time I wasted,
        wandering around in the darkness,
        blind to today's preciousness,
        wanting what I don't have.

Please show me the truth of this life
  and who you made me to be.
Show me the playfulness and joy that I seem to have
  lost over the years.

In our busyness and our effort-driven lives, it is so easy to lose that sense of who we are and Whose we are; it's so easy to begin defining ourselves by our titles, our work, and our roles. I have a suggestion, however, for a way to get to the bottom of it: try describing yourself by the way you love to play.

Think about it: I could tell you that I'm a teacher, a mother, a daughter, a wife—all noble roles. You would probably discover these things upon meeting me, because you would ask about my work and my family. But much more revealing is a list of things I like to do for fun. For instance, I love to dance. If you let me dance, I have enough energy to dance all evening; I don't even want to eat when I can dance! I also love playing games: loud, rowdy, physical games. I love to read, and I have relationships with my books. They are like my children. My playful self tells you a lot more about my heart than my job does.

Try describing your friends by the way they play. I know people with desk jobs who love to backpack; police officers who are musicians; mild-mannered bankers who turn into screaming fanatics at football games; administrative assistants who are clowns.

Even if your job sounds terribly exciting—say, you're an astronaut—we can still tell a lot about your heart when we find out what you're doing when you're fully engaged in your playful side, doing whatever it is that brings your joy to the surface.

Next time you meet someone for the first time, instead of asking, "Where do you work?" or "Do you have children?" make your first question, "So…what do you do for fun?"

And know that you'll know them better for having asked.

TRY THIS

Describe yourself as you would to a new acquaintance. Then write down all the things you love (or would love) to do for fun, and write a short description of yourself based on that. Compare. Be amazed at the way you come to life in the second description!

Come Together

4

BUDDY UP.

Why do women go to the bathroom in groups? I frequently hear men ask this question, and I have thus far been unable to come up with an answer that makes sense, other than, "It's just more fun that way." Which sounds pretty twisted unless you realize that, although everybody needs personal space, the advantages of gathering together often outshine going it alone.

Take my brother, Ted, and me, for instance. I adored him when I was little and thought he knew practically everything. (He was a great purveyor of valuable information, such as "Robbers live in your closet.") So when he decided to take his magic act on the road (he, starring as The Magician, the illusionist, the David Copperfield of the '60s), I begged to be his assistant. This important job consisted of him getting all the glory and me being what pretty much amounted to a servant. When he would clap his hands twice and shout "ASSISTANT!" I would instantly appear from offstage, bounding in to bring him whatever the next trick called for—usually from an expansive collection of scarves, magic wands, top hats, marked playing cards, fake rabbits, rubber chickens, and the like.

We played the usual places: old people's parties, family gatherings, old people's parties, church banquets, old people's parties, and—our most celebrated gig—the Bozo the Clown Show. Yes, we were actually on TV. It was heaven!

After a while, though, Ted became restless. Tired of pouring fake milk into trick glasses, he was anxious to move into the bigger leagues. He decided one day—after watching one too many illusionists on TV—that he was ready to try some serious levitation…and I was to be the levitee.

I was ecstatic. I could hardly wait to levitate, even though I didn't know what it meant.

When I found out that he was going to suspend me in mid-air, I backed off a little, but then decided it was better than being sawed in two, so I consented. He did explain to me then, that we were just going to give the *illusion* of suspending me in midair. All we had to do was figure out how.

And after some thought, he came up with a plan.

First, I was to lie down on the piano bench. He then found two yardsticks for me to hold, one in each hand with my arms at my sides, and a big shoe to put on the end of each yardstick. Then he draped a blanket over me so all you could see was my head and these enormous clodhoppers sticking out the other end

When he shouted, "ASSISTANT…RISE!!!" that was my cue to crane my neck up toward the ceiling while simultaneously lifting the yardsticks with the shoes on the far ends, so it would appear I was suspended mysteriously in midair.

We thought it was a fine trick and quite convincing. But when you do a run-through for your parents, and you finish and turn around only to see them with their faces all contorted, which you know to be a sign of repressed laughter, it certainly knocks the wind out of your sails.

We always considered it one class act that never quite made it big. However, making it big is not a prerequisite for having fun.

Ted and his older friends also let me be in the neighborhood "plays" that they wrote and performed for their parents in our neighbor Phil's basement. The only one I actually remember was a work of art called "The Funny Farmer." I do not recall who the farmer was or why he was considered to be so funny, but I do remember pestering the big boys to let me participate. Finally, they relented and let me be the girl who walks across the stage with a huge sign that says, "Act 1," "Act 2," and "THE END." I loved it.

You can also learn things when you're having fun with others that you would never discover on your own. For instance, when you were young, didn't you have a friend who knew more about everything than you did? This was usually the kid who knew about "female matters" before your mom thought you needed to know, or before they showed you "the movie" in the fourth grade. (In our school, all the little boys were sent out to recess while the little girls were mysteriously herded down to the cafeteria for some "girl time." Of course, despite heroic efforts by the faculty to keep the little boys from peeking in the windows and figuring out what was going on, the boys usually had an inkling that it had something to do with "reproduction," whatever that was in their little minds, and they teased us mercilessly about it after school.) Anyway, my friend Debbie was the one in the know before me, so I always had fun when I went to her house and got the scoop on the mysteries of life.

One day we were playing with our Barbies and Kens—my favorite dolls of all time. We had put the Barbies down for naps, because they were tired. Or so I thought. Apparently *her* Barbie wasn't tired, because out of the corner of my eye, I saw her raising Ken way up in the air, and then dive-bombing him down directly on top of Barbie. I was mortified. "What in the world are you *doing*?" I asked her, completely puzzled by this sudden violent act. "That's what your mom and dad do *every night*," she announced, with great satisfaction, especially when she could see that I was totally grossed out. "Ewww!" I squealed. "Not *my* mom and dad!"

This was one time I was sure she was completely off base, because I had never had any indication that my father was in the habit of sailing through the air and landing with a thud on top of my mother. I mean, please. Their room was right down the hall from mine. This is something I would know.

Since neither of us had a clue about what was supposed to happen after that, I think Barbie and Ken got up and had a cookout or something. We had fun the rest of the afternoon, but I couldn't get that crazy "flying Ken" picture out of my mind, so when I got home, I asked my mom about such things. Though I never did tell her what prompted my questions (she'll find out when she reads this), it was the beginning of some good dialogue between us about the facts of life.

The fun you have when you team up with a friend is priceless. Not always worth a lot maybe, but priceless just the same.

By nature, many women are prone to clump up and collaborate, socialize, or, as I mentioned before, go to the bathroom. Generally, we are good at inventing excuses to do things together, mainly so we can talk, like girls' night out, women's retreats, and shopping trips that require chartered buses so we can, you know, go as a group. Women even group up at the end of beauty pageants to "congratulate" the winner. (I was never convinced as a child, however, that that's really what they were doing at the end of the Miss America pageant. I remember thinking that the losers were all surrounding the winner to beat her up.)

So I really shouldn't even have to remind women that teaming up with another person or a group really is worth the effort on occasion. However, there may be a person or two who needs to be reminded that teaming up can double, triple, or even quadruple the amusement. It's just that we're so busy, and arranging to get together takes time and effort and calendar coordination. However, where two or more are gathered, you can have a kind of re-creation that you wouldn't dream up on your own.

There's a reason the apostle Paul gave new believers this advice: *"Let us not give up meeting together, as some are in the habit of doing, but let us encourage one another"* (Hebrews 10:25). Believers in Paul's day did not have an easy time of it in a world that was so new to the teachings of Jesus. He knew that they needed one another to share heavy loads and to laugh till their sides ached; he knew the value of surrounding ourselves with comrades—both in large groups and a close inner circle—for the creative learning, encouragement, and spirit lifting that happens among friends. He knew—and so do you—that God doesn't intend for us to do this life alone.

TRY THIS *What kinds of fun have you had when you teamed up with one or more friends? Is there something you'd love to do with them that you just haven't made time for yet? Corral those cattle, and head out!*

MIRROR, MIRROR

5

H ave you ever done something destructive in the name of fun? Many people have, at one time or another, which is ironic, because fun isn't supposed to hurt at all; it's supposed to be liberating and... well...*fun*. But most of us have probably been guilty of gossiping or teasing some kid who was different in some way. As we grew older, the damage may have involved alcohol or drugs or sex. Regardless of the type of your destructive "fun of choice," you probably found out pretty quickly how abusing your freedom to choose by choosing the wrong thing actually takes the freedom away and locks you up—physically, emotionally, relationally, and spiritually. Always

FORGIVE
YOURSELF.

a lazy little goof-off at heart, I learned this the hard way at the tender age of five.

I loved sweets, especially Dum-Dum suckers, and used to sneak them out of the candy dish in the kitchen and off into the living room, where I ate them while I watched TV. Knowing that I would get into trouble for my contraband food, though, I had to be creative in hiding the evidence—the sticks and wrappers. This required a little trial and error in my mind: Should I stuff them between books on the bookshelf? No good. You could see that the books weren't closing all the way. Should I shove them under the couch? That would be okay, as long as my mother never ran a vacuum cleaner there. She often did, however.

Finally, I came upon a brilliant plan. My parents' bedroom was right off the living room, and the door was conveniently located close to the TV. On the back of the door hung a full length mirror: the perfect place to hide the evidence! I was jubilant, because I figured that I could probably hide wrappers and sticks behind that mirror till I graduated from high school, and no one would be the wiser.

Of course my mother discovered them one day and told my father, and he called my brother and me into the living room for a confrontation. Since my brother, Ted, was six years older than me, knew everything, and was innocent of the crime, I decided that I'd follow his lead in responding to Daddy's interrogation.

"All right, who did this?" he asked, looking us over for incriminating facial expressions.

"I didn't do it, honest," said Ted.

"I didn't do it, honest," said I, doing my best to look wide-eyed and innocent.

I could tell he was surprised that neither of us was willing to confess, and I wondered what on earth Daddy would do about it. Punish us both? Or take a guess and punish the more likely liar, since he had a fifty-fifty chance of convicting the real criminal? The last thing I expected him to do was what he did.

Nothing.

After a minute of looking back and forth at us, he simply said, "Okay," and he let us go.

I couldn't believe it! I was off the hook! Guilty, but not charged!

Life was good...for a while...about five minutes, maybe. I then started to feel as guilty as I was. All day I avoided Daddy at all costs, my heart pounding. Around two in the afternoon, I was playing (okay, *hiding*) in my bedroom, when he appeared in the doorway. He only wanted to ask me something entirely unrelated to The Deed, but as soon as I saw him, my guilt reflex kicked in. In a panic, I threw my hands up in the air like I'd been caught robbing a bank, and shouted, "I didn't do it, honest!"

I think this is what tipped him off.

Still, he said nothing to me about the matter; he only wanted to know how I was doing.

I lasted about three more hours: three more hours of beating a hasty retreat out of whatever room he entered; three more hours of explaining to Barbie and Ken why I was forced to tell an untruth to my father; three more hours of imagining the spanking to end all spankings that would surely be mine if I owned up. Finally, around 5:00 P.M., I could stand the tension no more. I would confess, I decided, because anything was better than this distance I had put between Daddy and me, not to mention the anxiety that was destroying every effort I was making to have a Saturday of quality play.

Nervously I tiptoed into the kitchen, where he was sitting at the table with my mom. Before I could say a word, he motioned me to come to him. Bracing myself as I made my approach, I thought, "This is it. I've been had. I might as well gear up for the spanking of my life." To my surprise, though, instead of turning me over his knee, he picked me up, set me in his lap, and whispered in my ear, "Why don't you tell Mommy it was you who put those sucker sticks behind the mirror?"

At that invitation, my heart burst, and I cried tears of relief, confessing that I was the one who did it and deserved to go to jail. Fortunately, he didn't think jail was warranted; he just let me sit on his lap till I calmed down. Then he took my hand, led me into the bedroom and said, "Why don't we clean up this mess together?"

Even though it was considerable work (I *had* done a magnificent job of sticking and stuffing!), I didn't mind. My relationship with my father was right again, and that's what mattered most to me.

That day I learned that there is only one solution for fun gone bad—for life gone bad—and that is forgiveness. And I've always been grateful for the simple act of grace Daddy gave me, because even all these years later, I replay that day in my heart, and it still reminds me of God's promise and John's declaration: "*If we confess our sins, he is faithful and just and will forgive us our sins and purify us from all unrighteousness*" (1 John 1:9).

I love thinking that God, too, invites us—whether we've messed up at six or sixteen or sixty—to come to Him, and even sit in His lap, as He whispers in our ear, "Why don't you just own up to that colossal misjudgment you made? You'll have to clean up the mess, but I'm here with you. I forgive you."

And with that forgiveness comes freedom—freedom to forgive yourself, to move on, to know real joy, and to make sure there's plenty of quality playtime—for the little goof-off who may live inside you too.

TRY THIS *Think about the destructive things you've done in the past to have "fun." If you haven't already, ask God's forgiveness. If you need to list them and burn them, do so.*

The Hills Are Alive

6

Are there any movies from your childhood that you just can't forget? Depending on how old you are, you might remember *Old Yeller*, or Hayley Mills and Hayley Mills in *The Parent Trap*.

The movie that made the biggest impression on my young life, however, was *The Sound of Music*. I remember being completely fascinated with the whole setting....

Those hills! How did Julie Andrews get all the way up there by herself? Wasn't she supposed to be somewhere, like at work or something? And how come she never got dizzy, with all that turning around in circles while she was singing?

That strength! As she was making her way up to the Von Trapp home for the first

BE ACTIVE RATHER THAN PASSIVE.

time, singing "I Have Confidence," I marveled at her ability to hurl that suitcase around.

The romance! What young girl didn't dream of being Liesl cavorting around the gazebo with Rolfe, singing "Sixteen Going on Seventeen," leaping from bench to bench in the rain, he in his manly little uniform and she in that magnificent twirly dress? I wanted that dress.

The rainstorm! I delighted in watching Maria try to distract the children from the thunder and lightning by dancing around the bedroom, hopping on the bed, weaving in and out of the curtains, singing about raindrops on roses and...well, you know, all that other stuff.

The goofy outfits! Maria made these for all the children ("Play clothes," she called them. Was she *joking*? No kid I knew would make it off the playground in one piece with those get-ups on.) out of curtains—strangely reminiscent of the trick Scarlett O'Hara pulled in *Gone with the Wind*...only Scarlett didn't get the idea while she was darting around the bedroom. And Scarlett's dress looked a lot better than the play clothes, too. Nevertheless, I was fascinated by anyone's ability to clothe eight children using window coverings. I went home and stared at our own living room drapes, trying to imagine what kind of "play clothes" my mom could have made me. Then I envisioned her ripping the drapes off the curtain rods, valances flying, whisking the material to the sewing machine, and whipping up a pair of lederhosen for me to sport on my Saturday trips to the dump with my father. Somehow it just didn't work in real life.

But never mind. I adored the movie anyway. It stimulated my little brain to many such flights of fancy, as I imagined myself a Von Trapp child singing "Do Re Mi" with my brothers and sisters, jumping around on the steps of gorgeous European buildings, and hiding in a cemetery to escape the Nazis.

So you can imagine how thrilled I was when, as an adult and not that long ago, I had the chance to see it on the big screen...

and this time with an added bonus. The Sing-Along Sound of Music came to a city near me, and I will never be the same.

I almost didn't go. It was a weeknight, and I was worried that we wouldn't get home till late, blah, blah, blah. But the opportunity to go with a group of friends and actually interact with my favorite childhood film was too much to resist. Here's how it worked: The original film was to be shown with words to the songs at the bottom of the screen. We were not only encouraged to "follow the bouncing ball" and sing along, we were also practically commanded to participate with the actors themselves, by offering (shouting) any commentary on the action that might come to mind. Since most people in the audience had memorized half the dialogue anyway, there was a lot they felt compelled to say.

But I get ahead of myself. When we entered the theater, we were given a goodie bag that contained a piece of curtain fabric, an invitation to the ball, a party popper to pop when Captain von Trapp kissed Maria at last, and a sprig of little white flowers—Edelweiss—to wave around when they sang the song by the same name. Examining these treasures was only the beginning of the fun.

I also noticed that many folks were outfitted very strangely for the evening—a fact that made sense when I found out there was a costume contest. People were dressed up like every imaginable detail from the movie: a fair number of Marias and nuns, of course, but also brown paper packages tied up with strings, drops of golden sun, dogs biting, bees stinging, gazebos, and, my favorite, a girl with "16" on her shirt, riding piggyback on a fellow with "17" on his shirt. Next time I will dress up, too... probably as a curtain.

Anyway, an emcee came out to coach the audience on their part in the evening's fun. We were to sing along with the songs, of course, but also feel free to provide commentary on the action. For instance, he told us that, as the film opened, we

would see nothing but hills. At this point, we were to start yelling, "Where's Maria? Where's Maria?" and in a little while, a dot would appear on the screen. As soon we saw the dot, we were to point and shout, "THERE she is!" The music would then swell, Maria would come into view, start turning in those circles, and we would all start to sing, "THE HILLS ARE ALIIIIVE...." It cracks me up just to think of it.

We participated all through the movie: we booed the bad guys, hissed at Baroness Schraeder, and cheered and popped our party poppers when Captain von Trapp finally kissed Maria. We shouted out lines before the actors could say them, and added a few of our own. When the Von Trapps were hiding in the cemetery, having to be perfectly quiet, some audience member's cell phone rang. "I hate it when that happens," someone else yelled.

All in all, it was great fun to actually see how much noise you could make in a movie theater. Granted, it takes a certain kind of personality and a certain obsession with *The Sound of Music* to truly enjoy an entire evening of uninhibited stupidity like that. I had to think about why this kind of event was so appealing to so many people, though. I believe there's something about being an active participant in fun for fun's sake; totally absorbed in the moment, especially in a community of people who are also committed to uninhibited stupidity...or at least being totally absorbed in the moment.

It was so different from sitting passively and being "entertained" for the evening. The movie, in fact, was only part of the entertainment. The audience—with the singing, props, costumes, and comments—was the heart of it, and that active participation turned a night at the movies into a party like no other.

Maybe you have been guilty, at some time, of sitting on the sidelines, passively watching others have fun, wanting to participate, but contenting yourself with being a spectator. Maybe you were afraid of looking silly or of failing, or maybe you thought that active participation was just too much trouble. Mostly, though, you knew that you regretted sitting on the sidelines.

If that's the case, you'll be happy to know that Jesus was and is a proponent of being proactive. He even encourages us to come to God this way: "**Ask** and it will be given to you; **seek** and you will find; **knock** and the door will be opened to you. For everyone who asks receives; he who seeks finds; and to him who knocks, the door will be opened" (Matthew 7:7; bold added for emphasis). I love the fact that Jesus actually invites us to ask for what we want; to look for God and His answers; to knock on His door, beat on it even, knowing He will open it and invite us to come on in. And if this attitude of action is a good way to approach the Creator, I have to believe that He designed us to be proactive about the rest of life as well—even in fun.

TRY THIS

Think about the times when you sat on the sidelines while others were having fun; you wanted to participate but chose not to for some reason. Now, in your mind or on paper, replay the scene, this time with you taking part in the fun. Maybe you have thought about initiating some fun—getting a group together for a movie or visiting a new coffee shop or taking in some live music—and just never got around to doing it. Make a list of activities you have thought about organizing. Post it where you can see it, and just do one of them.

JOY IN THE MORNING

7

REMEMBER.

Leonard Sweet says in his book, *Learn to Dance the SoulSalsa*, "If you are not constantly recalling back to life meaningful memories and stories, your soul is being starved to death.... Memories fall to the ground and fertilize the soil so that the soul can grow."

When friends or family members gather, a lot of entertaining, if not embarrassing, memories are often bandied about. And if your family and friends are like mine, we love to share them over and over. They never seem to get old, unless you are a teenager and the recollections are about how cute you used to be. Usually, though, it's a great kind of fun to recall the goofy things you did as a kid...or a teenager...or maybe last week. It wasn't until recently, though, that I thought of memories as "soul food," too.

Maybe memories of your past, particularly of your child-hood, are painful; maybe they are idyllic; maybe, like mine, they are some of both.

One of my favorite recollections involves my father. I was very much a daddy's girl growing up and used to love the rituals we had. Every Saturday, we had a habit of going to a very special place, a place that came to be "ours," a place that I would always, even as an adult, associate with fun and security: the dump. The dump was simply the best. Mountains and mountains of trash and stinky stuff, it's true, but also endless piles of fascinating junk were ours for the taking. Actually, we rarely took anything back home, but the time spent hanging around the landfill with my father was priceless to me.

Also, on every other Saturday, he and my brother would let me come to the barbershop with them. This was especially fun, if not a little frightening, because the barber himself was bald and always offered to give me a haircut, which I usually declined. I did, however, accept his bubble gum, which, looking back, wasn't all that great—not the soft kind with the little comic strip in it, but the cheap kind, the kind that was tough as concrete and would pull the fillings out of your teeth. Still, my brother and I ecstatically chewed the stuff because, hey, it was free.

Christmastime was the best. I loved listening to Christmas albums on our huge stereo—a gigantic piece of furniture, big enough to hide two men and a small boy. My favorite, the one with Johnny Mathis on the cover with his skis, got scratched up from constant playing, but we never replaced it; we just sang along with the scratches. To this day, I can only sing "Winter Wonderland" this way:

> Sleigh bells ring, are ya (SCRATCH) nin';
> In the lane (SCRATCH) glistenin';
> A beautiful sight, we're happy (SCRATCH) night;
> Walkin' (SCRAAAAAAAAAAAATCH) onderland

I also love thinking about how I used to sit on his lap, suck my thumb, and rub his right ear because it was fuzzier than his left ear. I can tell you what he smelled like when he came in from cutting the grass. He actually let me push the mower once in a while. He woke up in the morning by smoking Chesterfield cigarettes and drinking coffee at the kitchen table. He was appropriately amazed at my ability to play the piano and twirl a baton (not at the same time). Why, he actually wanted to be in the delivery room when I was born, which was rare in the 1950s. Family vacations with him as chief navigator were the highlight of every summer.

On one trip to New England when I was ten, however, Daddy got sick. This meant my brother, who had turned 16 about two weeks before, had to drive home. Not good news for me; I was so frightened of my brother's neophyte driving, I used to lie down in the back seat so I couldn't see what was heading into our windshield.

Much to my relief, we got home in one piece anyway and called the doctor. After a brief examination, he said that Daddy had food poisoning and should be okay in a couple of days. I remember that night, praying that God would make him feel better the next day; then, confident my prayers would be answered, I rolled over and went to sleep.

The next day, the doctor stopped by (this was a small town!) and pronounced Daddy much improved; he *was* acting like he felt a little better. So that night I thanked God for answering my prayers from the night before, asked Him to keep up the good work, and, in continued childlike faith, rolled over and went to sleep.

The next day, my brother woke me up, telling me they'd had to take him to the hospital, but not to worry, that everything would be okay. However, when a family friend knocked on our door and asked us to come with him to the hospital, I knew something was very wrong. Whimpering to myself as I got dressed, I wanted to know what was going on, but was afraid to ask.

We pulled into the emergency room exit and went into a private sitting room. There, my mother sat in a chair, weeping and surrounded by friends.

She looked up at me and said, "Daddy's gone."

"Gone?" I thought for a split second. "Gone where?"

But I knew exactly what she meant. The universe collapsed.

Gone were the trips to the dump. Gone were the trips to the barbershop. Gone was the only man on earth who thought I was amazing and beautiful in all my chubby ten-year-old attempts to twirl a baton and play the piano. Gone was the nice, safe life we knew as a family.

Five months later was our first Christmas without him—and aren't those "firsts" the worst? They have to top the list of days you'd like to erase from the calendar if you could. We had my aunt and uncle over for dinner on Christmas Eve. Asparagus casserole was on the menu for the evening, and I hated asparagus casserole. But the worst part of the evening was that my daddy wasn't with us, and I knew Christmas would never be the same. I knew life would never be the same. What used to be the happiest, most secure place on earth now felt empty and tentative and sad…unbearably sad.

After dinner, I sat in my bedroom in the dark next to the window. The sky had turned loose, and instead of magical, beautiful snow falling, it was pouring down rain. I remember watching it beat down on the sidewalk outside, thinking that God and all creation were crying with me.

Perhaps you have felt the same, and wondered, "Where is the joy in life, when you feel that even God is crying with you?"

Maybe it is tucked into a memory.

I know. Sometimes remembering hurts, especially when grief is raw and new…and sometimes even when it's been around so long, it's just part of your every day. But sometimes,

after a time, you find yourself remembering and smiling instead of weeping.

My own soul is fed every time I remember my father in his undershirt, with a microphone in his hand, singing, "Give me some men who are stout hearted men!" into a gargantuan reel-to-reel tape recorder we used to have; I receive more soul food when I think of him throwing his arm around my mother in the front seat of our Rambler station wagon, singing, "Ridin' along in my automobile...my baby beside me at the wheel!" I also remember growing up into awkward adolescence without him, but with the sure knowledge that once upon a time I was some-body's princess, and feeling that in some way, I always will be.

Maybe your soul, too, will be fed when you realize that the life of the one you're missing hasn't really left you at all but is waiting to surprise you, like an old friend who visits just when you need reassurance that memories don't die, even if people do.

Maybe you will allow yourself to be comforted by reassurance from the psalmist:

> *Weeping may remain for a night,*
> *but rejoicing comes in the morning.*
> —Psalm 30:5

And maybe you will be able to echo David's sentiments when he says,

> *You turned my wailing into dancing;*
> *you removed my sackcloth and clothed me with joy,*
> *that my heart may sing to you and not be silent.*
> *O* LORD *my God, I will give you thanks forever.*
> —Psalm 30:11–12

When you are missing someone, go ahead and miss them with all your might. Grieve, and know that things will not be the same without them. But know, too, that they will always be a part of who you are, and let your heart dance with the joy they brought—and still bring—to your life.

Don't forget to remember your own trips to the dump. And smile.

TRY THIS *If you have lost a loved one and are finding it hard to have fun, try writing down good memories. Save them in a special place, and as you revisit them, you may cry, yes...but also pay attention to the parts that make you smile.*

STORIES FROM

ADOLESCENCE

IN [BRAD'S] COLD BLOOD

8

I have a theory about fear in relationship to fun—namely, there are two kinds: (1) the kind where you say to yourself, "I'm really scared of this, and I *do not* want to do it," and (2) the kind where you say to yourself, "I'm scared of this, but I really *do* want to do it." In general, my advice is don't do the fearful thing if you really don't want to. As for the second kind? Go for it.

We all want to live fearlessly—not with a stupid kind of fearlessness that moves God to shake His head and say, "What is she *thinking*, trying to jump a motorcycle across Niagara Falls?"—but a fearlessness that trusts God implicitly and allows us to open ourselves up to life free of neurosis.

**MOVE
PAST
YOUR FEAR.**

Two little boys gave me some pointers on having a good time without fear when I was in the seventh grade. I was a bit nervous about taking care of Brad and Jeff, since this was my first babysitting job. However, my mom was right across the street, so I could consult her if emergencies came up, like potty training or the Heimlich maneuver.

Their mother, Mary Kay, had been my babysitter when I was little, so we were old friends, and she trusted me far more than I deserved to be trusted.

Before Mary Kay went off to work the first day, she gave me a list of instructions. She said that the boys were allowed to play in the fenced area between the garage and the house. (They lived in an upstairs apartment in the house with a good view of that part of the yard.) So in the middle of the day, when the boys wanted to play down there in the sandbox, I took them down, positioned them in the sand, and then ran up the stairs to make their lunch. I checked on them frequently to make sure they were behaving, and they were. But shortly after the third "behavior check," I heard a crash…then raucous laughter. Naturally, I ran to the window to see what was going on.

And what to my wondering eyes did appear? Two little boys who had somehow jiggled the locked door to the garage open and had found a veritable treasure trove of glass bottles there. They were tossing them up into the air just to watch them land with a crash on the sidewalk; then they were shrieking with delight and scurrying back for another round.

I, on the other hand, was consumed with fright…and with good reason. I tore down the steps and into the yard, only to see that Brad, who was happily tossing his last bottle up in the air, was covered with blood. I grabbed him, shouted at Jeff to follow me, ran back up the stairs into the apartment, and started to wash him off so I could figure out where this profusion of blood was coming from. The whole time, he didn't even act as if he were hurt—only annoyed that I had interrupted his fearless fun. He looked at me as if to say, "What's a little blood when you can watch glass shatter into a million pieces on the sidewalk? Cool!"

As it turned out, he had a couple of small cuts—the kind that aren't very big, but bleed like a severed artery. After cleaning him up and lecturing them both on the dangers of partying with broken glass, I gave them lunch and put them down for a nap. During that quiet spell, I tried to figure out how I was going to tell their mother about what a lousy babysitter I had been.

When they awoke from their naps, I helped Brad get dressed and brought him into the living room...where Jeff wasn't. I went back to his room to see if he'd gone back to sleep. No Jeff there. In the bathroom? Not there. The kitchen? Nope.

About this time, my entire 13-year-old life flashed before me. I checked the yard again to see if he had escaped back to Glass Land. Not a trace. I called...and called...and called. Finally, I saw a clue: the window in the kitchen was open. So I ran to it, threw it open wider, and saw Jeff sitting on the roof of the house playing house builder. Not wanting to alarm him, I tried to cajole him back inside. "Jeffy," I said sweetly, "it's dangerous out there. You need to come back in." No response. So I had to crawl out on the roof and retrieve him. Like Brad in the previous unfortunate incident, he was not afraid, just disappointed that, for the second time that day, I had ruined his good time.

When I got them back in the living room, I felt like chaining them to the sofa. Instead, we had a lockdown in the truest sense. They became my prisoners for the rest of the day, while I prayed that God would spare my life when I told Mary Kay what happened.

Shecamehomethatafternoonandcheerfullyaskedhowourday went. "Well," I said, "Brad-and-Jeff-got-into-the-garage-and-broke-glass,-and-Brad-was-bleeding-but-he's-okay-now,-and-Jeff-got-out-onto-the-roof-through-the-kitchen-window,-but-aside-from-that-everything-went-just-fine!" Then I braced myself for a termination of employment. Instead, she just said, "Wow...well, boys will be boys!" Merciful, merciful woman.

In addition to learning a lesson in grace that day, I learned about fearlessness. True, Brad and Jeff's fearlessness was paired with indiscretion—not a good combination—but I envied their ability to plow ahead into uncharted territory without hesitation.

You may have found that, as an adult, you've developed more fears than you had when you were younger—fear of trying new things, fear of looking ridiculous, fear of something bad happening to someone you love—and this fear sometimes keeps you from plowing ahead into your own uncharted territory. Maybe the fear of flying is keeping you from visiting a far-off place, or a fear of water is keeping you from learning how to swim, or a fear of Montezuma's revenge is keeping you from taking a mission trip.

I actually have a fear of living my life in fear. How weird is that?

We must consider, though, that we may be doing ourselves and our God a disservice by not trusting Him with our fears. When God gave Joshua his instructions for leading the Israelites into Canaan, he actually *commanded* Joshua to push past his fear: "*Be strong and courageous. Do not be terrified; do not be discouraged, for the* LORD *your God will be with you wherever you go*" (Joshua 1:9). And to Joshua's credit, he forged ahead into some wild adventures, including crossing the Jordan River at flood stage. Had I been an Israelite in his charge, I would probably have suggested that we investigate the feasibility of building a bridge or, at the very least, a canoe. But God told them that once the feet of the priests carrying the Ark of the Covenant touched the water's edge, they'd be good to go. And they went.

Because they went, we have a vivid picture of what God can do when we move past our fears to follow His lead. And since the Bible states, "*the* LORD *your God will be with you wherever you go*," I believe that even in our play, He can certainly give us a taste of His power to inspire courage, if we'll only push forward and let Him.

TRY THIS

Have you ever declined an opportunity for fun because of fear? What could you do to overcome this fear? On the other hand, have you ever pushed through your fear to go on and do it anyway? Were you glad? What are you afraid of doing, but really want to do? What's to keep you from pushing through? Take courage and do it!

time to *go to bed* and put your head on the pillow?"). I couldn't wait for them to see the spider. I imagined them catching sight of it, screaming in terror, and beating it to a bloody pulp with a shoe or something. Oddly enough, I have no memory of them ever having any reaction to even one practical joke we attempted to play.

Grandma Pinney, however, was a different story. Since Grandma thought we were perfect, she believed Ted when he told her that someone (he probably blamed it on me) had ralphed on her carpet, as he had strategically placed the fake puke right outside the kitchen door.

She came out, took a look, said, "Oh boy..." and hustled off to get a rag to clean it up while we little goofballs were pounding the floor, thinking it was the funniest thing we had ever seen.

As I grew into adolescence, my brother instructed me in an art that I continue to enjoy to this day: toilet papering. Some people call it TP-*ing*; we call it *rolling*. My first experience with this art form involved a set of ground rules: First, you roll the houses of only the people you love, and you never do it as an act of malice. And since this is not to be an act of malice, you should never roll a house if the sky threatens rain. This would be just flat-out mean, since extracting wet toilet paper from trees takes years. You either have to call the fire department or let it biodegrade.

Anyway, when I was a teenager, Ted consented to teach me how to roll a house properly. We started with our preacher's house, because we loved him so much. I'll never forget the thrill of crouching in the bushes, bounding around the yard, learning how to snap my wrist just so to send a roll flying over the roof and down the other side of a house...and, best of all, finishing up and admiring a job well done. It looked like a snowstorm had hit the house in July. Just beautiful.

After that, I was hooked and went on to roll several more houses of people I loved. And only one time, when our buddy didn't realize that we were friends (as opposed to enemies)

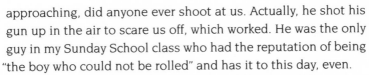

approaching, did anyone ever shoot at us. Actually, he shot his gun up in the air to scare us off, which worked. He was the only guy in my Sunday School class who had the reputation of being "the boy who could not be rolled" and has it to this day, even.

Anyway...since then, I have rolled dozens of homes of people I love. Sometimes we do the outside, sometimes just a room inside. (The trick here is to find where they hide their toilet paper—people have taken to hiding it when I come over for some reason—and roll them with their own paper so you don't have to go out and spend your own money.) One time, we persuaded a friend's son to give us the house key so we could roll the entire inside of the house while our friend was away. Oh, it was magnificent when we were finished.

I have also rolled offices and other work spaces, cars, and other inanimate objects belonging to someone I loved. The key is to remember that this is an act of affection, and you must make sure the person knows that if you didn't love them, you would not spend the time and effort to shower them with this artistic attention. In fact, that is the key to all truly successful mischief making: affection, not malice.

It also pays to be a little careful, however. Consider the case of my friends Fred and Ethel (names have been changed to protect the innocent): Pranksters that they were, they decided it would be fun to take a sponge cake to their friends, Lucy and Ricky. And I do mean a sponge cake, as in made out of a real sponge. They cut the sponge to look like a layer cake, iced it up with some chocolate frosting, placed it on a decorative plate, and brought it to their friends as a gift. Then they waited a few days for a response.

In the meantime, Lucy and Ricky had some friends who'd had a death in the family, and, as we all know, the first response of most people to death is "bring food." They were short on time and decided to take Fred and Ethel's beautiful untouched "sponge cake" to the grieving family as a sign of their care and concern.

Days passed. When Fred and Ethel finally could stand it no longer, they asked Lucy and Ricky how they liked the "sponge cake," to which Lucy and Ricky had to confess, "Well, to be honest, we gave it to the grieving Cleaver family...."

Fred and Ethel, appropriately mortified, told them the whole story, to which they responded also by being appropriately mortified...and they all wondered what in the world the grieving Cleavers were thinking of their crass sense of humor. When they finally got the nerve to apologize, they found the Cleavers to be most forgiving, if not fairly confused for awhile.

All that is to say, mischief can be enormous fun, but only if (1) nobody gets shot at, (2) you don't "regift" food that comes from a questionable source (Fred and Ethel *did* have a reputation for practical jokes), and (3) you play tricks that inspire laughter on people whom you are certain will actually laugh.

Surely somewhere in the Bible, there must be a few verses about the benefits of getting into mischief; however, I haven't found them yet. Look up *mischief* in a concordance, and you'll be referred to subjects such as *assault, calamity, misery, punishment, ruin,* and *trouble.* But I'd like to redefine the term here by directing your thoughts to Solomon's wisdom in Ecclesiastes 3. You may be very familiar with his reminder that there is a right time for everything:

There is a time for everything,
and a season for every activity under heaven:
a time to be born and a time to die,
a time to plant and a time to uproot,
a time to kill and a time to heal,
a time to tear down and a time to build,
a time to weep and a time to laugh...
He has made everything beautiful in its time.
—Ecclesiastes 3:1–4, 11

In the midst of the dying, uprooting, killing, tearing down, weeping, and mourning that you may be experiencing, remember that here and now, waiting for you, there is also birthing, planting, healing, building, and laughing. My prayer for you is that someday you will fall in a heap in a yard belonging to beloved friends, laughing, after you have felt the divine tension of trying to finish rolling their house while they sit blissfully unaware in their living room, watching TV.

I am certain that if you ask Him, God will be happy to show you the beauty of laughter during this time of your life—especially if it involves a little mischief.

TRY THIS *Is anyone among your friends and family known for their practical jokes? Tell a couple of these stories. Have you ever played a practical joke on someone as a sign of affection? If you can't remember the last time you did this, isn't it about time you gave someone who needs a laugh this kind of special attention?*

NAKED WITH CANDY

10

If you've ever watched children play, you know that they typically have no trouble forgetting everything else in their lives and getting lost in some unconstrained fun. And it seems that the younger they are, the more liberated they feel and act.

Writer Beth Levine tells this story about her little boy:

> Our son decided that not only was underwear objectionable, the rest of his clothes were as well. I found him running around the house stark naked, only pausing long enough to grab a treat from the kitchen table.

BE UNINHIBITED AND SAVOR SWEET OPPORTUNITIES.

"Mama!" he cried with soul-soaring glee. "I'm naked!
Naked with CANDY!"

"What more can you ask from life?" she asked her
husband. "I feel like being naked with candy myself."

—Beth Levine, "Mr. Wonderful" (Woman's Day,
February 18, 1997, p. 144)

It sounds tempting...and no wonder. It's the freedom that
we all long for: to be completely ourselves—no pretense, no
masks, nobody to impress, and nothing to hide. This liberated, "naked" state of mind, coupled with candy (the act of play
itself)—having something available that is sweet and delightful,
something that feeds us and exists for no other reason than to
bring pleasure—this is the essence of play.

I've often wondered what is it about adulthood that eats
away at our ability to cut loose and have some fun, especially
when I hear people say:

"I wish I were in high school again."

"I'd give my right arm to be in college again."

"The happiest times in your life are when your children
are little."

"These are NOT the golden years."

"Oh, to be [20, 30, 40, 50, 60, even 70] again."

It's not that I don't see some truth in all of these state-
ments...but I also see the tragedy in each one. Yes, life in
general gets in the way of our play, for the longer you've lived,
the more you've suffered, seen, and lost.

But I know when I allow myself to be unself-conscious and
willing to latch onto a sweet moment, life is infinitely more fun.
I actually did this once. And I was actually naked.

I was 19 years old and a counselor at a church camp for middle school kids. They were a fun bunch, especially since I wasn't
that much older than they were. But several of the counselors
were young, like I was, and always looking for adventure, even

at church camp, even in a position of responsibility, even when impressionable children were in our charge. It was our job to see that the children stayed out of trouble and wore their "swimmer" or "sinker" tags around their necks, especially in the lake. (How humiliating to be labeled a sinker. I should know. I had had to wear the tag nine years earlier at the same campground.)

Ah, camp—the land of cinder block cabins, community showers, and mosquitoes big enough to saddle up and ride into town. I loved it as a kid, despite being labeled a sinker and beginning what was to be a long career as a sleepwalker. One night, my counselor woke up to the tune of me trying to drag her out of her bed, telling her that "Everybody's in mine, and there's no room for me!" On another occasion, I wandered into the woods in the middle of the night looking for the bathroom that was actually in my cabin, two feet from my bed. So it was only natural that I would want to come back as an "adult" to help other preadolescents through the rites of camp.

One day, a bunch of us female counselors and the camp nurse thought it would be fun to sneak out of our cabins when the children were asleep in the night, and run down to the lake to go skinny dipping. I had never been skinny dipping before, and it sounded adventurous. So that evening, we synchronized our watches, made sure all the kids were asleep, met down at the water's edge, hid our clothes in the woods, and jumped in.

I have never felt such freedom in my life.

The moon was reflecting off the lake, and I couldn't resist taking the opportunity (this is the candy) to find the lifeguard's chair, climb up in it, thank God for such a stunning night, yell "BUDDY CHECK!" and leap into the water with…well, with soul-soaring glee.

This does not mean that I endorse shirking responsibilities to go participate in some risky, irresponsible stunt. Heavens, no. I mean, one of our kids could have had a medical emergency and had no one to take her to the camp nurse—if the camp nurse could even have been found. After all, she, too, was in the middle of the lake playing "Marco Polo." Furthermore, had the camp director caught us (he was a nice man, but very strict and extremely old—at least 40), we would have been banned from church camps all over the world forever. So, absolutely, I am not saying that taking a risk of this nature is something I would recommend doing.

What I *am* saying is that…well, to be perfectly honest, I'm glad that I had the experience of complete freedom one night one summer when the moon was full, the sky was loaded with stars, and God ever-so-benevolently decided to keep me from hurting myself.

I can honestly say that I know how Beth Levine's little boy felt when he was not only unself-conscious, but had the chance to grab the sweetness of a celebration of life—even if it was only for a moment—and run with it.

And I believe that this is what Paul had in mind when he urged the Philippians to "*Celebrate God all day, every day. I mean, revel in Him!*" (Philippians 4:4 *The Message*; bold added for emphasis). I love that phrase: "Revel in Him." Take intense satisfaction in Him. Be in the moment with Him. Because whatever else is happening in your life, I feel certain there is candy on your kitchen table right now, today—something sweet for you to celebrate, something begging to be reveled in. Feel the freedom (even with your clothes on), grab it, and run.

Today, right now, what can you celebrate in your life? Take this very moment to catch it before it leaves your consciousness, and start your celebration by thanking God. Then, feel free to include others in your party.

TRY THIS

FUN STUFF THAT ISNT ALWAYS

11

H ow often do people tell teen-agers, "Enjoy yourself! These are the best years of your life!"? I know this is true for some people; a few have even told me they would go back to being teen-agers in a heartbeat if they could.

Not me, brother.

It's not that my teenage years were so bad; I actually did have a significant amount of fun. However, the typical adoles-cent mind spends a lot of time anticipating Big Things and Big Events, and Big Things happening at Big Events. Unfortunately, this time of life is also full of Big Letdowns when you don't make it to the Big Events and the Big Things don't materialize. For most people, the reality of adolescence—

ENJOY
THE PROCESS.

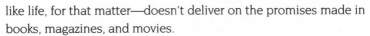

like life, for that matter—doesn't deliver on the promises made in books, magazines, and movies.

For instance, I exited my preteen years thinking that all teenagers date. And that not only do they date profusely, but they also all fall in love regularly. And if they don't fall in love, at the very least, they all get kissed before they graduate.

Here are some other myths:

Cruising is fun. Okay, cruising can be…for a while. However, when you've been at it for a couple of hours and fail to find the action you were hoping for, you park your vehicle and hope the action comes to you.

Sitting in the Pizza King parking lot (or the IGA parking lot at the other end of town) on Saturday night is fun. Actually, hanging out in parking lots on Saturday night only *appeared* to be wild, raucous fun. We were all just wishing we were somewhere doing something exciting—like on a date, getting kissed before we turned into pumpkins at graduation.

Dancing is fun. As I recall, high school dances were not 1950s jitterbugging contests, where people had steps to do and actually had some prescribed activity for their hands and feet. That would have been fun. But by the time I got to high school, we just sort of jumped around on the dance floor and did our own thing, which is extremely uncomfortable for some people who believe everyone is watching them and thinking how awkward and uncool they look. Many people just stood around, trying to appear cool, with the guys too nervous to ask anyone to dance and the girls going home disappointed because no one asked them to dance. Or worse, the guy they wanted to ask them asked someone else to dance.

Dances are fun. This is largely a myth that was confirmed to me when I went to pick up my daughter after a middle school dance once. I arrived earlier than the pickup time and slithered into the dark gym, trying to be invisible. At least three times in a half-hour period, I saw a small herd of chattering girls migrate to the bathroom, surrounding one weeping girl and offering consoling phrases such as, "What a creep! He's no good for you anyway!" Each time, it was a different chattering herd and a different weeper, but the scene was the same. Some fun they were having. (Just for the record, the boys were all pasted against the wall on one side of the gym. They, too, were having the time of their lives.)

The prom is supposed to be the Most Fun Night of Your Life So Far. Granted, for some people, the prom works. We try so hard to make it the Most Fun Night of Your Life So Far (the dress, the tux, the flowers, the hair, the limo, the pictures) that we often set ourselves up for disappointment.

I was no exception to this natural law.

I was desperate for a date to the prom my senior year—so desperate that my friends Steve and Nancy had to actually import a date from another country, because there were no viable local takers. Of course, they felt as though Foreign Young Man needed to be introduced to me before the big night, so they arranged a cozy little blind date for the four of us at a little burger joint across town.

I was terrified. I learned that he had asked Steve what I looked like, and Steve replied, "Well, she's no Miss America, but she's a lot of fun!"

Talk about the kiss of death. I just knew he would try to escape once he got a look at me, and I'd miss out on my prom, the biggest night of my senior year and possibly my entire existence.

However, he did not try to escape. We had a lovely time silently smiling at each other across the table, since he spoke only a smidgen of English. But that was fine with me, because I was going to spend the next couple of weeks engaged in one of

the most exhilarating processes of my young life: getting ready
for the prom. The preliminaries to this life-changing event, of
course, involved lots of phone time with my girlfriends, talking
about where and how we'd get our hair done and what kinds of
dresses we wanted. And though getting my hair done (that is,
paying someone to tease and spray and sculpt it into a prom-
worthy helmet) was a thrill, the best part by far was shopping for
formal wear. And since, like many other young girls, I had always
thought that on prom night, you should be pretty much feeling
like a princess, my expectations as Mom and I set out for the
nearest mall were high.

Clothing miracles didn't usually happen to me; but when
I spotted a particularly magnificent piece of finery in the window
of Nobbson's, I knew it was mine. I pointed, claimed it for my
very own, ran into the store, grabbed it off the rack, rushed into
a dressing room, slipped into it, and emerged on Cloud Nine.
And what a vision I was in those huge puffy sleeves, lace that
obviously didn't know when to quit, and row upon endless row
of blush-colored crinoline that poofed out into a gigantic skirt.
Thinking back on it now, I believe I must have looked a little like
Cinderella gone bad, wearing a great pink marshmallow that
had exploded into a dress. I adored it, though, so much that it
still hangs in my closet today!

When Foreign Young Man picked me up on the big night,
I was ready to have the time of my life. I floated to the car, sat in
the front seat, and ended up with a large portion of that large
dress in my face. But that was okay, because I knew my date was
dazzled. Besides, we were on our way to the ball.

The dance floor was already crowded when we arrived, and
we wasted no time in joining the fun. To my delight, I quickly
learned that no matter what country he came from or how much
English he couldn't speak, he could certainly boogie American.
I was unaware, however, that my delight was about to turn to
disillusionment. After a couple of songs—a little Blood, Sweat

and Tears, a little Chicago—he jerked his head toward the door and uttered his first completely English phrase: "Do you want to go to parking lot?"

Naively, I thought, "Parking lot? Did I leave something in the car? Was there a fire in the building? Was there something going *on* in the parking lot? Was there…ohhhh! Go to the parking lot and…. Oh man, no, I didn't want to go to the parking lot and do *that*" (whatever happened to be on his mind)!

The rest of the evening, we spent dancing, with him nudging my arm and asking me every half hour or so if I was *now* ready to "go to parking lot." Obviously, I reasoned, he must have misinterpreted Steve's definition of "a lot of fun."

The good times rolled downhill from there. Since we weren't communicating on the same wavelength, we stopped communicating at all. The rest of the night was, frankly, boring. He took me home early. I was completely disappointed and convinced that my entire adolescence had climaxed into a dull thud.

The truth is that I had a lot more fun *getting ready* to go than I had actually *going* to the event. Getting my hair done, shopping for a great dress, and talking with my friends about how it was going to be the Most Fun Night of Our Lives So Far were the fun times. As I look back on that night, I'm thankful I appreciated the journey to the ball, since there was a considerable lack of bibbity-bobbity-boo once we got there.

Shame on us (and we've all been here) when we are so consumed with the end product—the special event, the prize, the task all finished—that we forget to enjoy the view along the way. Because, let's face it, by the time we psyche ourselves up for the Big Thing, it may have morphed into a monster, making it practically impossible to be all it was cracked up to be in our overachieving little minds.

Most of us need frequent reminders to enjoy the present for all it's worth. In Matthew 6:33–34 (*The Message*), Jesus assures His disciples that God has the future in His hands, and that it's important to *"Steep your life in God-reality, God-initiative, God-provisions."* Then *"Give your entire attention to what God is doing right now."*

Think about it: right now is all we have anyway, and since what He's doing right now is pretty spectacular, we're going to miss most of it if we barrel through the process with blinders on. The good news is this: it's not too late to enjoy this moment, and the next, and the next, until one day, you look back with satisfaction and realize that you actually enjoyed the journey, full of God Himself—even if a few of your destinations were fun stuff that wasn't really.

TRY THIS

Getting ready for a big event or even a small event? Don't forget that the process is just as important—and often even more fun—than the result. Make a sign that says "Enjoy the process!" and post it where you'll see it every day.

ASKING BOYS OUT

12

Many mothers (maybe yours) have told their daughters that it's not ladylike to call boys on the phone and even worse to ask them out. Fortunately, I never considered myself particularly ladylike. I was forced to really work for just about every date I ever had.

I actually got pretty good at it, since I was in a girls' club in high school that had two functions every year—a banquet and a dance—and if you wanted to go, you *had* to do the asking. Starting my freshman year, I tried a variety of techniques; the first was to approach "Larry," a buddy, claim that I had two "extra" tickets to a banquet, and ask him if he wanted to go. It worked.

SOMETIMES GOD WORKS THROUGH FUN.

For the next event, I worked up to asking "Curly," a guy I actually had a huge crush on. There is, of course, much more at stake when you put yourself out there for someone who makes your palms sweat, but I was determined to go to this dance with somebody I liked—and I mean "liked" liked. So I called him. I could tell that I caught him off guard, but he said yes. Ecstatic, I started making plans. Two days later he called me, and said he couldn't go after all. Something about having to wash his hair.

I was crushed, but not destroyed.

Determined to get back on the horse, I called "Moe." By this time, though, my self-confidence was waning. I worked up the nerve to dial the number...but hung up after the first ring. Gathering myself together, I tried again...and hung up after the second ring.

"Okay, this is just dumb," I told myself. "Do you want to go to this dance or not?"

"Yes, yes," my wimpy self answered.

"Then just do it," my brave self commanded.

So I dialed the number. The phone rang once...then twice. Moe's little brother answered. "Could I speak to Moe?" I squeaked in a barely audible, not to mention trembling, voice. "Surrrrrrrrre," said Little Brother, who then covered the mouthpiece and, in an evil, singsongy little falsetto voice said, "Moooooooooe! It's a girrrrrrrrl!"

I couldn't help it. I hung up.... And then I called Larry, claimed that I had two extra tickets to a dance, and asked him if he wanted to go. It worked again. Believe it or not, this went on for *four years* until the senior prom (see "Fun Stuff That Isn't Always").

At the time, I believed there was something terribly wrong with me; now I see that God was preparing me with experience and courage for a shot at some fun that would change my life.

When I got to Purdue University, I lived in an all-female dorm that—wouldn't you know it—had a dance every year. If you wanted to go, you had to ask. As in high school, I was determined not to let a little threat of rejection keep me from the fun of my own dance. In my junior year, I had a big crush on a friend—an adorable boy with long hair and ratty jeans—and decided that I needed to go to this big event with him. So I began working up the nerve to ask him. I actually worked on this nerve for a solid month, since attempting a leap from "friend" to "more than friend" is potentially ego damaging.

One evening, we were in a meeting together, when I decided to just paint myself into a corner. "When the meeting's over," I told him, "don't go away. I need to talk to you."

Do I need to tell you that I had no idea what happened in that meeting? I just endured it, as I sat there with my palms sweating profusely (as when I thought about Curly during my high school years). When the meeting finally ended, we went back to my friend's room in the grad house.

By this time, he could tell I was nervous and, being a rather cocky boy, he was actually enjoying it. He took the only chair in the room (leaving no place for me to sit except the edge of the bed), put his feet up on the desk, folded his arms across his chest, and said, "Now...what was it you wanted to ask me?"

This irritating attitude actually made me a little mad, but I just told myself, "Play it off, girl, just play it off."

So I said, "Buddy, I'm about to give you the opportunity of a lifetime."

"And this is?"

"To take me to a dance."

He laughed. I laughed.

And eight weeks later, he asked me to marry him.

Of course, I said no.

Then much later, I said yes.

Then I said no again.

Then I said yes again.

But that's another story.

The point is, we've been married for 30 years. I've asked my husband, Ben, repeatedly why, if he liked me enough to try to get me to marry him after eight weeks of dating, didn't he ever *ask me out*. He has never given me a satisfactory answer, which tells me, plain and simply, he was just chicken (see the Moe tale).

I will always believe God's hand was in my heart, giving me the desire (and the practice!) to start the ball rolling. As with many attempts to have fun, this one took a little nerve. I have a framed greeting card sitting on my desk that says simply, "No guts, no glory"; it explains our story well, and serves as good advice, too. When God gives you a prompting in your gut, I think you should pay attention to it. Even if it's for fun, He may have a greater purpose in mind, some bigger plans, *"for it is God who works in you to will and to act according to his good purpose"* (Philippians 2:13), and it is God *"who is able to do immeasurably more than all we ask or imagine, according to his power that is at work within us"* (Ephesians 3:20).

Sound a little over the top? Not in my book.

TRY THIS *Has God ever used your desire for fun and joy for a greater purpose than just for your own fun and joy? Share this with a friend. Has He put in you a desire recently to have some fun that could be used for a greater purpose?*

ANIMAL HoUse

13

Rocky, the big lumbering golden retriever who belongs to our neighbors Ron and Freda is, I am convinced, the original inspiration for the term *party animal*. Maybe you know a dog like him.

Although he is no longer young and not exactly the picture of canine physical fitness, Rocky has been on the hunt for a good time for many years. One day, he retrieved and deposited at Ron and Freda's doorstep a few venison bones and a bottle of barbecue sauce. Another morning, Ron came out on the porch to find a pizza box and a beer bottle. But Rocky's best efforts were showcased one evening when he came trotting home with a crock pot full of Brunswick stew in

HANG OUT WITH NONHUMANS.

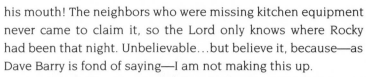

his mouth! The neighbors who were missing kitchen equipment never came to claim it, so the Lord only knows where Rocky had been that night. Unbelievable…but believe it, because—as Dave Barry is fond of saying—I am not making this up.

Rocky's "port-a-parties" only reinforce my belief that animals can add infinite pleasure and excitement to your life, not to mention a steady supply of bounty from a neighborhood hunt.

As I was growing up, our home always seemed to have one animal visitor or another. Once a bat decided to take up residence in the fireplace and then make himself at home in our living room. I believe my father used a broom to "persuade" him that life outdoors was better for his health. Then there was the squirrel who dashed into our kitchen just in time for lunch one day; we, in turn, dashed around the room, slamming all the doors shut, watching the poor thing freak out as he frantically looked for a way to escape. I believe the bat's broom helped him find the escape route.

Because we lived in front of a cornfield, we always had plenty of mice, which I hated. Even though mice are tiny and shy and furry—all prerequisites for a good pet—they gave me the creeps, skittering around like little cowards, leaving calling cards in inconvenient places. One night in particular when I was a teenager, I had a small conniption when I pulled down my bedspread and discovered a little grey lump under my blanket. Of course, I screamed. (Why I screamed, I don't know. Was he capable of hurting me? Did I expect him to leap from the bed in a vicious attack?) I ran into the kitchen, yelling at Mom, "There's a *mouse* in my bed! Oh gross! How did he *get there*? Pleeeease go get him and take him away!" And my mom, ever fearless, took immediate action. Our usual weapon of choice, the broom, seemed too gentle for this quick and evil little creature, so she went for the hard stuff: a hammer. Yes! She would smash his little skull, and he'd never know what hit him.

I chose to stay in the kitchen, unable to witness the violence. So Mom crept down the hallway to my room alone, hammer poised over her head. Gingerly, she pushed the door open, tiptoed in and, with the furtive skill of a stealth bomber, approached her target. Then, *wham!* I heard the hammer hit the bed once…twice…and a third time. I waited for her to emerge with a lifeless little body; instead, she came out laughing. As it turns out, when she lifted the blanket, she found that she'd just beaten the living daylights out of one of my hair curlers.

Real pets, however, are a different story. Pets can be lifesavers. I am fascinated by stories of animals warning their masters of impending disaster, dialing 911 in medical emergencies, and dragging children out of harm's way. Unfortunately, I have no experience with heroic rescues of this type; our pets were never especially bright, but they did provide us with hours of entertainment and great joy. When Blackie, our favorite cocker spaniel, gave birth to puppies at the same time that our cat of the month gave birth to kittens, we were in heaven. They all slept together in the doghouse. We would have slept in there with them if there'd been enough room.

The pet that fascinated me most was Goldie, a cat I got when I was 14. Goldie was the original cat with attitude. She was pretty nice as long as you were doing what she wanted. You could have her in your arms and she'd be perfectly happy, purring away. But as soon as she signaled a sinister mood change with a low, menacing growl, you had about ten seconds to turn her loose, or else "Cat Scratch Fever" would become more than a song.

Despite that little flaw, however, I loved her for her spunkiness. One day she came to the back door with a little present for us—not the usual rabbit remains, but a little bird, still very much alive and fluttering. Of course, *someone* opened the door, Goldie opened her mouth, the bird flew in the house, and my quick-thinking mom chased it into her bedroom closet and slammed

the door. Which seemed reasonable for a split second, until she started wondering how she was going to get it out of there.

She was furious with Goldie, so she decided to turn the dirty deed over to the culprit. I will never forget the sight of my mom, by then Mad Mary, as she grabbed the cat under one arm and marched down the hallway to her bedroom, saying, "You brought that bird into the house, *you* can get rid of it!" And she shocked us all by tossing the cat into the closet with the bird and slamming the door shut.

I was mortified, but fascinated as we listened to the violent thumping and whacking sounds. Eventually, they stopped. We opened the door, and sure enough, Goldie had won that battle. Mom was impressed.

When Goldie got pregnant, we were thrilled at the prospect of having kittens around. Okay, I was thrilled. Unfortunately, she was due to deliver right around the time my brother was to get married.

Mom had made a little bed for her in our basement—our cold, dark, creepy basement—certainly no place to be in the most significant travail of her life. So the day before the wedding, I accidentally on purpose left the basement door cracked, so she could rest in the house until it was time to deliver downstairs.

My poor mother was too exhausted to notice, because she was having the rehearsal dinner at our house. With all those people coming for a meal and the stress of a wedding the next day, she pretty much wasn't paying attention to anything else. That night, after we'd cleaned up and were ready to fall into bed, I wandered into her room for a book and noticed a little lump under the bedspread. This time it wasn't a mouse… or a hair curler; it was alive and mewing. Yes, Goldie was giving birth—messy, beautiful birth—in my mother's bed. I was riveted…elated…and *terrified*, because I had to tell Mom.

I preferred the coward's way out and just asked her to come into her room. You can imagine her reaction. "I thought she was in the basement! How in the world did she get up here? I shut the door, and...." And she knew. And miraculously, she was too tired to beat the tar out of *me*. Instead, we just set about stripping the bed down to the box springs and taking Goldie and her kittens downstairs. I was moved to tears at the sight of her giving life to five tiny balls of wet fur, and felt unusually close to God that night because I was certain that I could see Him in the face of that mama cat.

I love the fact that God saw fit to birth His Son into our lives most likely in the middle of the company of animals. If you've ever spent the night in a barn, you know the sweet/sour pungent smell of hay and manure and the peaceful night sounds of animals snuffling and snorting and rustling; you may even recognize the bleating of sheep or lowing of cows. It is raw and earthy and so close to creation and the Creator. When I read that Mary wrapped Jesus in swaddling cloths and placed him in a manger (Luke 2:7), I love to imagine the same peacefulness, the same fragrance, the same donkeys and sheep staring wide-eyed, wondering what was up with the baby in their feeding trough.

It was no accident that God chose for Jesus to be born among the creatures who have the ability to comfort us, to help us keep life in proper perspective, to amuse and fascinate us, to give us a listening ear. Whether they are domestic pets, farm animals, or wild things that you have the privilege of watching on safari, on a hike, or in a zoo, they often take us out of the world we've made for ourselves and into the natural world He made for us.

TRY THIS *Have you ever found God in the gift of animals? How? Start looking for Him! Even if you have no pets or dislike pets, it's fun and therapeutic to watch them.*

eaT YouR CaKe AND HaVe FuN WITH IT Too

14

I began to not eat like a normal person in the summer I was 19. That was going to be the summer, I decided, when I would finally lose weight. Not just a couple of pounds, mind you, but significant weight. I set my sights on a number that was 20 pounds less than the weight the scale registered the first week of May; then I began a long journey toward wrecking my relationship with food.

Although I could have joined a weight loss group or chosen any of a number of other ways to lose weight, I, of course, wouldn't consider a *reasonable* method. For pity's sake, why be reasonable when you could be radical and stupid? So I counted calories, setting my daily limit

PLAY WITH YOUR FOOD.

at 900. I memorized my calorie counter and tested my mother's culinary creativity (as well as her patience), as I ate practically nothing for breakfast, lunch, and dinner. In an effort to get a little something sweet, I remember putting liquid sweetener on dry toast. Yuck!

For ten weeks, no dessert passed my lips—nothing fattening, nothing fun. I woke up every morning angry, because I knew I was beginning another day of deprivation. But, by golly, I was dedicated to it. In a couple of months, I had lost 20 pounds, all right…and a significant portion of my mind with it.

Before school started, I was so desperate to be nondeprived, I actually looked with lust at a few stewed prunes my mom was cooking on the stove. Prunes, I knew, though good for you, were not exactly low in calories, so I tried to point my mind in another direction. But alas, it didn't work—it was like trying *not* to think of pink elephants. Before I knew it, I was frantically retrieving every prune in the house and throwing them in a pot of heated water. Indeed, I thought they were magnificent—which is very sad. Even as I write this, I think about how sick it is to finally bust out of a diet with something like stewed prunes. Before my whole food orgy was over, I had eaten 26 of them.

Yes, that's right. I ate 26 stewed prunes. Do I even need to explain why I had to plead "sick" the next day?

Shortly after that, it was 32 chocolate chip cookies. Another time, the Reese's peanut butter cups that were in the freezer were calling my name. I ate 125 of them in five days; that would be about 25 a day for five days in a row. Obviously God, in an act of grace, had given me an asbestos stomach.

As unfortunately happens with many young women, I was stuck in a deprivation mind-set that wouldn't let me go. I began starving myself during the week, then eating so much on the weekends that I would end up physically ill. Although I was never anorexic or bulimic, I was always either empty or overfull. It was a crummy place to live.

By the time I got married at age 22, I was tired of my bizarre relationship with food and was determined—for the sake of my body, my husband, and our future family—to eat like a normal person. Unfortunately, that required cooking, and I couldn't guarantee that I would learn to *cook* like a normal person. This was ever so obvious when I decided to whip up some navy beans for Ben one day. I knew they were good with ham, and so I asked a friend about what kind of ham to use. "Ham hocks are best," she said. Ham hocks? I was too embarrassed to admit that I didn't have the faintest idea about what a ham hock actually was, so I said, "Oh yeah, ham hocks. Why didn't I think of that?" And I scurried off to the grocery store in search of one.

Once there, I rang the butcher's bell and asked him to show me a ham hock that was worthy to be put in a pot of beans; when he led me over to the meat cooler and pointed at this grotesque-looking piece of pig leg, I wanted to cry. But I figured if I was going to have to cook Southern, I might as well bite the bullet with a ham hock. So I bought it, took it home, and took it out of the package. To my complete dismay and revulsion, I discovered that this piece of meat actually had *hair* on it! H*air*! The stuff that, should you find it in your dinner at a restaurant, causes you to choke, send your food back, and wait hopefully for a free meal because of it. This was too much. Was I going to have to cook meat with hair on it? And this was no baby-fine, angel hair, either. These hairs were black and wicked and coarse and nasty. Well, I was way too embarrassed to call my buddy to ask what to do about this problem, so I did the only thing I knew how to do.

That afternoon when Ben came home, he saw me intent on the task. "What in the world are you doing with the pig's ankle?" he asked.

"Tweezing it," I said, as though I did this every day when he went to work. "You don't want hair in your food, do you?"

That, my friend, is *not* having fun with food—no more fun than 26 stewed prunes. But I *do* think I deserve a few points for taking a whack at it.

I am still not the world's greatest cook (see "Turkey Bird"), but I have since learned a few lessons about how much fun you can have with food.

Eating should be fun. I hadn't realized how little we pay attention to our food in our hurry to consume it until one semester when I had a European student who described in his journal his daily eating experiences. He said he always took 30 minutes for breakfast and another 30 for lunch. Then, he and his roommate always bought fresh ingredients for their meals, such as vegetables, fruits, and breads...and they took a full 45 minutes to eat dinner, which, for college students, is some kind of record. But, as he said, "You Americans...you eat too much, too fast." And he's right. I knew I could consume 26 stewed prunes in about 20 minutes. I envied him and vowed to do the same. But it's so hard.

A friend of mine was playing hostess to two exchange students from France. One evening was especially hectic, as she was chauffeuring her daughter around and doing errands. Before a meeting that evening, they needed a quick dinner, so she stopped at a fast food drive-through. The exchange students were awed. "We've never eaten in the car before," they said. Mealtime for so many of us has become something to get out of the way so we can get on to the next thing.

But tell me, is there anything better than a relaxed meal during which you actually taste everything? When you sit around the table for an hour or maybe even two afterward just talking and enjoying the company? When the meal itself is worthy to be considered an event? It certainly doesn't have to be anything fancy; the only requirement is time to enjoy it.

Maybe you were told not to play with your food when you were a kid, but I am asking you to consider erasing that tape in your mind. Who hasn't thoroughly enjoyed "plowing a field" in

the mashed potatoes with a fork? (Or is that something only kids from the Midwest do?) And it's usually early in life when we learn that practically anything edible that comes out of an aerosol can is fun (whipped cream, cheese product). Also, anything you can construct to look like something else is fun. One year at Christmas, my brother and I actually made a pig's face (complete with ears and a 3-D snout) out of the ham slices on my mom's meat platter (and we have pictures to prove it). Remember Pop Rocks? Now they were fun, and there was nothing to the rumor that said if you ate them and drank a carbonated drink at the same time your mouth would explode...much to my disappointment. And then there's the king of all fun foods: Jell-O. Oh, the crazy things you can do with food that wiggles.

Even the method of eating can add enormous enjoyment to the experience. Eating with your hands is fun. Eating outdoors is fun. Eating stuff cooked on a stick is fun.

It's an incredible gift from God, this food we have to eat. The writer of Ecclesiastes recognized it when he advised his subjects to enjoy their lives as much as possible; to "*Go, eat your food with gladness, and drink your wine with a joyful heart, for it is now that God favors what you do*" (Ecclesiastes 9:7). Apparently, in his day as well as ours, it was so easy to abuse food, ignore it, and forget that God made it for our nourishment and, yes, even our fun. With the exception of stewed prunes, which in my opinion He created for one purpose only, our relationship with every other food can and should be an exercise in thankfulness, creativity... and even playfulness.

TRY THIS *What is your relationship with food these days? Is eating just something to get out of the way so you can go on to the next thing? Do you abuse food, eating out of stress or distress? Think of some ways could you celebrate food and enjoy it more this week.*

STORIES FROM

YOUNG ADULTHOOD

GLAMOUR SHOTS

15

GET OVER YOURSELF.

The desire to look good seems to drive us to all manner of odd activity, even when we are very young, and especially when the looking good involves putting on a little razzle-dazzle. When I was little, my cousin Marilyn and I got matching "mink" stoles and plastic high heels for Christmas; we were in heaven. We also used to dig into my grandmother's hamper full of her old dresses and pocketbooks and play movie star, stuffing all kinds of rags into bags and tying them onto our behinds to act as bustles under the dresses she let us wear. The reason we actually felt compelled to make our behinds bigger escapes me now. When I think of it, I can only imagine how Grandma must have felt as she watched us "load up" just to fill out her old clothes. Still, our efforts to put a little glitz and glamour into our otherwise conventional little lives remain some of my favorite memories of play as a child—efforts that continued, for me anyway, well into adulthood.

One year, I thought it would be fun to surprise Ben at Christmas by getting my picture taken at one of those places that purport to make you more glamorous than you have ever been or will ever be again in your life: sort of an adult dress-up opportunity. I made an appointment and arrived at the studio in the mall, ready, willing, and really looking forward to a temporary ultimate makeover.

They were very busy that night and in the process of training a new photographer—a girl who had, up to that very evening, been a makeup artist only. This made me nervous right out of the gate because I am a bad study for even a great professional photographer. I wear glasses, for one thing, and I discovered long ago that I have some kind of quirky thing going on with my left eye. Without fail (even in my wedding pictures), that eye shuts just as the camera shoots. Also, I have hair with a mind of its own (I wake up in the morning, look in the mirror, and ask it what *it* wants to do).

The hairstylist tamed the wild beast the best she could, the makeup artist shoveled cosmetics on, and the wardrobe lady gave me several binding, sequin-studded denim numbers. They were the kind of outfits you find on a frivolous shopping trip, pull off the rack, hold up to yourself, and holler at your friends, "Hey, what about *this* one?" and then convulse into laughter, because you know you would *never* wear the thing in real life.

Then I very carefully (so as not to break, lose, or fall out of anything) took a seat in front of the camera, where the new photographer immediately made a terrible mistake: she tried to convince me to take my glasses off.

"But I won't look like myself!" I protested.

"That's the idea," she said.

We went back and forth over that one for a few minutes; I eventually won out. But two hours and several bizarre twists of the head and neck later, I was sitting in the front of the studio viewing the proofs on a screen when I felt hot breath on the back of my neck. It was the manager, staring at the shots and shaking his head.

"You don't have much to choose from there, do you?" he said.

I didn't know whether to commend him for being perceptive or yell at him for being rude.

Actually, he was right. Glare off my glasses was a problem in several pictures; I looked like I was positively poured into one glamour suit; and my left eye was half shut, of course, in most of the pictures, making me look as though I were a tiny bit tipsy.

"Tell you what," he said, without waiting for me to answer. "If you've got another couple of hours, you can have another sitting for free."

Free? These were worse than I thought.

So he sent me in to a more experienced photographer (the one they send all their remedial customers to, no doubt). And *four hours* after I first walked in, long after the mall had closed, I walked out with some priceless photos of me in a red feather boa (to match my glasses) and with both eyes pretty much open.

Had I not been equipped with a highly developed sense of humor, I would have pronounced that experience a disaster; however, if you have had enough fun in your lifetime, you know that a lot of it requires you to "get over yourself" as far as physical appearance goes. Unfortunately, we girls aren't always very good at it.

You know how it is. You probably can't even count the number of women you've known who will come to a gathering at the river, the lake, the beach, or someone's pool and not even put on a swimsuit. They will pass up the most delicious opportunity of the summer, all because they don't have perfect bodies. What is really going on here? Are we so self-absorbed that we think anyone actually *cares* that we don't look like Barbie in a swim-suit? My theory is that most people don't care what *you* look like because they're too busy obsessing about what *they themselves* look like, thinking that you actually care what they look like, which you don't…at all—if you know what I mean.

Mind you, just because I complain about this doesn't mean I don't relate. I do.

A few years ago, I was on a winter retreat with a group from our church. One evening, a friend excitedly told me that we could rent an hour in a hot tub, and they needed a sixth person to split the cost. Was I interested? You bet! At the end of a day on the slopes, nothing feels better than sinking your joints in some hot water—especially if you ski like I do: face first (see "Wonderland"). Plus, it would be so much fun with friends.

I was all set to run back to the room and put on my bathing suit, when I casually asked him who else would be there. "Oh," he replied, "Fab Abs, Flat Stomach, Killer Tan, Bodacious Behind, and Much Younger Than You." Actually, he said their real names, but somehow my mind processed them this way. Go figure.

I stopped right there and started to say, "Oh…uh…well…no thanks." The thought of being cloistered in a hot tub and com-pared with such perfection made me want to put on a really long flannel nightgown and go straight to bed. But then I thought about all the fun I'd be missing and decided that my own self-consciousness was not going to cheat me out of a good time.

So I went. I soaked. I had fun. And it was good.

Go, my friend, and do likewise…and be reassured by Peter's words as stated in 1 Peter 3:3–4 (*The Message*): *"What matters is not your outer appearance—the styling of your hair, the jewelry you wear, the cut of your clothes* [the way you look in a swimsuit!]*—but your inner disposition,"* a disposition that's big on celebration—not self-consciousness.

TRY THIS

Have you ever passed up on a chance for fun because it would make you look less than your photogenic best or because you would look less attractive than everyone else? Tell about this. Then replay the opportunity as though you couldn't care less about what you looked like. There, now—wasn't that a lot more fun?

HAPPY BIRTHDAY

16

B uying a birthday present for a man is probably one of the hardest things you will ever do. They just don't seem to ever *need* anything—at least not when you have to think about buying them something. Or they will play little mind games with you, like Ben does every Christmas when I ask him what he would like, and he replies, "Oh, I have a list in my head, and anyone who really knows me will know what to get me." That's it—the only guidelines I get. Then after Christmas, we'll be cleaning up, and he'll say, "Well, maybe I'll get what I wanted next year." This used to drive me completely batty until I figured out that he was just trying to aggravate me.

GET OUTSIDE THE BOX ONE WAY OR ANOTHER.

He wasn't kidding around, however, one year as his birthday neared. The only thing on his list—on our list—was a baby.

Our struggle with infertility was taking us on a heavy-hearted journey, our days filled with endless doctors' visits, lots of poking and prodding, reports of "there's nothing more we can do," and prayers that were not answered the way we thought God should be answering. And the nights—oh, they were the worst. During the day, we could at least be distracted by noise and work and busyness. But when nighttime came, we would lie in the darkness, nothing more to say to each other, on pillows wet with our tears, on a bed that used to be a refuge, a place where we would love and dream. But that bed, the house...even our love often seemed empty at night.

I desperately wanted to give him a present that would bring him (and me) some hope, some reminder that life could still be good, some respite from our pain and frustration. Fortunately, God helped me resurrect my sense of humor, even in this drought, so I decided it was time to muster it up and put it to work. I came up with a plan that was slightly bizarre, one that might put Ben's career in jeopardy, but would, in my view, certainly be worth a little risk: I decided to send myself to my husband.

A week before his birthday, I called a singing telegram company, Mr. Flim Flam, and arranged for the messenger to come to Ben's office and sing a special birthday song to him that I had written. Then I asked for a little teensy favor: "Um, do you think your messenger would mind delivering a package, too?"

The guy on the other end replied, "Oh, that's no problem."

"And there's one other thing...."

"Sure, what's that?"

"I'll be in the package, if that's okay. I thought I'd jump out after the song."

Silence.

"Will you have your clothes on?"

Well, *of course* I'd be fully clothed. What did he think I was, some kind of exhibitionist?

Rather reluctantly, he agreed to send the messenger to the lobby of Ben's workplace, where he would meet up with the birthday box. Now all I had to do was figure out how to deliver myself to that point.

For days I prowled around his office building (at the time, we, conveniently, worked for the same company in neighboring buildings that were attached by a walkway and a tunnel, so I knew exactly where to prowl), looking for a box big enough to hold me. At last, Lloyd, the typewriter repairman (this was a long time ago!) found a huge one for me. It took an entire lunch hour to figure out how to actually get me into the box without breaking my neck, but Lloyd thought the whole idea was so entertaining, he volunteered to be my accomplice.

It took another entire lunch hour to wrap the box like a birthday present, but we did it, laughing the whole time about how we hoped this didn't get us (and Ben) fired.

Finally, the big day arrived. We put the wrapped box on a big hand truck, Lloyd hoisted me over the edge, dropped me in, put the lid on the top, and proceeded to roll the whole thing through the tunnel and into the elevator to meet the telegram deliverer in Ben's building. If you've never been shut up in a box before, I will tell you that, for me, it grew more unpleasant by the minute. I am slightly claustrophobic (see "Cow Suit"), and sitting around in a fetal position in a small dark space is not my idea of a good time. After a couple minutes, I started to imagine all the things that Lloyd could do to me while I was in this box. He could pull the dolly right out the door and shove the whole thing down the steps of the building into oncoming traffic...or he could duct tape the lid onto the box as a joke, and I would never, ever see daylight again...or....

"You okay in there?" he asked, right before my imagination forced me to pop out prematurely.

"Oh sure," I said, just as I felt the elevator stop.

"Okay, here we are. We have to quit talking."

I could feel the wheels of the hand truck move, and I heard Lloyd and the telegram man exchange greetings and make jokes about the "nut case inside the box."

The telegram man took over, rolled me into Ben's office and started yelling his name which, as you can imagine, attracted quite a crowd. Then he sang the regular version of "Happy Birthday" followed by a second verse:

This message is clear
You got one last year.
But this time it comes with
This package right here!

As Ben took the lid off the box, I jumped out, gave him a big kiss, and watched his face, trying to read his reaction. "Deer in headlights" would probably describe it best...or maybe "deer in headlights with mouth hanging open" would be better. For a split second I panicked, thinking that this time I had finally crossed the line from "innovative and cute" to "dangerously dumb." But then he started laughing. *That* was a relief. Then I searched the crowd of onlookers for his boss to make sure *he* was laughing, which he was, and I knew I was home free.

What started out as a struggle to think of a fun birthday present became a milestone—not only in our memories, but in our marriage. Maybe your goal right now isn't to get pregnant (if it is, I don't recommend this as a fertility treatment). And maybe you're thinking that jumping out of a big box in front of a bunch of people is something you are unwilling to do this side of heaven...and maybe on the other side, too. However, what I did wasn't really about being an exhibitionist; rather, it was about being willing to do something a little unorthodox (okay, a lot unorthodox) that would give us both a wonderful break from our painful situation, if only for a little while. It absolutely worked! And now, 25 years later, we still laugh about it.

I like to think I'm in good company, since Jesus, too, was all about innovative perspectives. When John's disciples asked Jesus why His disciples didn't fast as the Pharisees traditionally did, Jesus explained to them that there was a time and a place to fast. Then He suggested to them that it was time to look at the former laws in a different way now that He was with them:

> "No one sews a patch of unshrunk cloth on an old garment, for the patch will pull away from the garment, making the tear worse. Neither do men pour new wine into old wineskins. If they do, the skins will burst, the wine will run out and the wineskins will be ruined. No, they pour new wine into new wineskins, and both are preserved."
> —Matthew 9:16–17

He was urging them to open their minds and hearts to His teaching, His new perspectives on the Law, and His out-of-the-box message about the grace of God—and He didn't stop with the disciples. He constantly asks the same of us, in all of life: to be willing to think outside the "wineskin"—the old one, anyway—and be open to His unorthodox intentions for our lives, whether we are in the midst of a personal drought or just trying to find a reason to laugh.

Do you know someone who needs a lift? Make a list of such persons in your life, and think of some ways you can provide that lift.

CLIMBING

17

PAY ATTENTION TO YOUR HEART

At one time or another, you have probably been struck with a case of the "buts." Typically, this starts when you see someone doing something—say, swinging on a trapeze—and say to yourself: "Wow, that looks like fun. I'd do that myself, but _____." Then you fill in the blank with an assortment of excellent reasons, such as, "I'm too old to swing on a trapeze," "I'm not coordinated enough to swing on a trapeze," "I would look dumb swinging on a trapeze," "people would think I was crazy to swing on a trapeze," or—the mother of all excuses—"I don't have time to learn how to swing on a trapeze."

I understand completely. I thought of all those excuses and more when I saw a women's rock climbing and rappelling trip advertised in a local university's newspaper. However, that time, my desire to do something adventuresome as I approached 40 won out over my hesitation.

I was proud of myself for signing up, but as the time for our first preparatory meeting neared, my apprehension mounted. I had seen pictures in travel brochures of people rock climbing: long, lean bodies in spandex, dangling from rocky heights. What if this group was full of 19-year-old cheerleaders/contortionists? What if I just wasn't fit enough to do this? What if I was too scared to try? And what was the name of the place where we were supposed to climb? Great *Falls*, Virginia? An ominous title, if you asked me.

By the time the weekend rolled around, however, I was full of high hopes. Friday we piled into the van, drove to our campground, and set up. That night it rained—hard. We got wet—real wet. As I lay in my soggy sleeping bag, I thought about Ben and our daughter, Jamie, at home. (In the midst of our struggle with infertility, we had been blessed with a daughter.) They were dry...in a bed...and looking forward to horseback riding the next day on terra firma.

But Saturday morning dawned clear and blue, and I found myself getting ready to rappel for the first time. A little nervous, I tried to understand the leader's directions, but all I could see was the small cliff in front of me. "Okay," she said after she hooked me up, "grab the rope in your right hand, lean back and let go." She had to be kidding. "I just want to show you that I can save you even if you pass out." *That* was reassuring. What if *she* passed out?

But she was right. And the extra measure of safety gave me the courage to lean way back into a sitting position in midair. I released the rope a little, then backed down; released, backed down. It was actually fun. I felt like Batman descending a sky-scraper wall in Gotham City—only this wasn't a camera trick. "Holy rappel ropes," I thought. "I'm actually doing this at my advanced age. Not bad."

Climbing, however, turned out to be more work. Especially since, as we were gathered for instruction, our leader said, "Okay, take out your bandannas."

Probably to tie around our foreheads to catch sweat, I thought. But no.

"Now," she smiled, "you don't have to do this if you don't want to"—I could feel dread wash over me, knowing that an enormous wave of peer pressure was approaching—"but I'd like you to make this climb blindfolded."

Ha-ha. I thought she said *blindfolded*. As in *blind*, unable to see. She couldn't have meant that...but she did.

"By eliminating your sight," she explained, "you'll be more attuned to your other senses, mainly the touch in your hands and feet." Personally, I would rather have been able to *see* my hands and feet, but as I said, the other eternally enthusiastic climbers all agreed that yes, it would be a wonderful thing, being attuned to your other senses, so I acquiesced.

I watched several others go first, until there was no more stalling. With a bandanna over my eyes, I started feeling my way up. Inch by inch and oh so slowly, I ran my hands over the rock. Lifting my feet, putting a toe on what felt like nothing bigger than a pebble, I was doing a vertical crawl. My arms pulled, my feet pushed, and my body balanced until I was halfway up. Then suddenly, I could feel nothing but smooth rock. I thought I had a toehold on something, but.... Oops!

"I'M FALL...,"I started to yell.

But before I could even finish my SOS, my leader pulled on the rope and held me. Gee, now I was one of those suspended in midair. Too bad I couldn't stay there.

"There's nothing to hold on to!" I yelled at no one in particular, thinking that I must look ridiculous, that I was too old for this, that I was no good at sports, and that I should be doing something more productive with my time, like cleaning the house.

But in response came directions from my new friends below.

"Jam that foot in!"

"Move to your left!"

"Good job!"

"You're almost there!"

Their encouragement kept me going, and finally came the blessed news: "You're at the top! Stop climbing and take your blindfold off."

First I looked down—and I do mean down—at all my encouragers, then out at the Great Falls of the Potomac, and then up at the magnificent sky. And I thought I heard the theme song from *Rocky* playing in my head.

That night I couldn't sleep, maybe because I was in the back of the van. (My sleeping bag was still soaked. I was cold, but at least I wasn't wet.) Mainly, though, I couldn't keep the day's events from dancing all over my thoughts. So I pulled out my journal and flashlight and wrote about how glad I was that I had followed my heart. It wasn't just the physical challenge that made the trip meaningful; it was also everything that surrounded that challenge:

- Trusting someone you just met to hold your lifeline.
- Trying to climb. Never mind if you couldn't make it to the top of every rock. Few of us could. Taking the first step was the biggest accomplishment.
- Coming back to camp, energized after a day's climb, to a lot of excited talk and a dinner of hot baked potatoes covered with fresh steamed vegetables and melted cheese.
- Taking a night hike in the woods, with the moon so full and bright that we didn't need flashlights. Stopping in the middle of that hike, in the middle of the woods, in the middle of the night, being very quiet, and feeling God's presence wrapping around me like a velvet blanket.
- Best of all, sharing my faith with a girl young enough to be my daughter.

On the bus trip home, we talked about her boyfriend and my husband. She had a lot of questions about how to know if this guy is the right guy and about how to make a relationship last, especially a marriage. When I told her we'd been married 18 years, she got this look of wonderment on her face and said: "Wow, that's a *long* time. What does it take to make a marriage last *all those years*?" Her tone of voice was the same as if she had said, "So what was it really like when you went to Abraham Lincoln's inauguration?"

In response to her questions, I had a great chance to tell her how important it has been in our marriage to share a common faith in God and His ability to help us overcome obstacles we couldn't handle ourselves.

For that moment and all the others, I have always been glad that I followed the calling of my heart and went on that trip.

In fact, I am convinced that part of the restlessness and sadness we feel in this life comes from *not doing what we are called to do*—in work, yes, but also in play. How has God called you to have fun? This may seem like a crazy question—but it's so necessary to ask and to answer. You need to find out what God has built you for, since the One who knew you before you were born is the One who knows you even better than you know yourself.

Jeremiah learned this truth when God called him to do a very special job:

> "Before I formed you in the womb I knew you,
> before you were born I set you apart;
> I appointed you as a prophet to the nations."
> —Jeremiah 1:5

In spite of God's reassurance that He knew the man inside and out and had therefore custom-designed this activity for him, even Jeremiah had—surprise!—a case of the "buts."

"'Ah, Sovereign LORD,' I said, 'I do not know how to speak; I am only a child'" (Jeremiah 1:6). Now that might sound familiar. You may even want to fill in the following blanks in several different ways: But God, I do not know how to _____; I am only a _____.

And God might well respond to you the same way he responded to Jeremiah: "Do not say, 'I am only a child.' You must go to everyone I send you to and say whatever I command you. Do not be afraid of them, for I am with you and will rescue you" (Jeremiah 1:7–8). Then God gave Jeremiah exactly what he needed to do what He had asked him to do, and finished the admonition by saying, "Get yourself ready!" (Jeremiah 1:17).

Of course, Jeremiah was gearing up for some very serious work—confronting the people of Judah with their sins. But I believe that in work and in play, God wires us up with deep desires that propel us toward our potential.

This is a question worth answering: What are you doing— in your work and in your play—when you think and feel, "I was made for this" or "God wired me up to love this"?

If you can answer that question and, even then, find yourself falling victim to a case of the "buts," I'd urge you to think instead, "Why not?" Why not take piano lessons, go on a safari, learn to belly dance, or even swing on a trapeze?

TRY THIS

What are you doing—in your work and in your play—when you think and feel, "I was made for this" or "God wired me up to love this"? "What," asks Max Lucado, "ignites your heart?" It's very important to pay attention to these thoughts. Write them down. Brainstorm a plan for acting on just one of these loves.

[Mess Up The] House Party

18

THROW
ONE.

I f the thought of throwing a party strikes fear and terror in your heart, you are not alone. Often, thoughts of entertaining are accompanied by nightmares about several things: (1) getting the house clean (Is there ever enough time?); (2) figuring out what to eat (This is always a dreaded task for me. I am a boring cook and not gifted at making what I call "cute food"—the little morsels that perch on top of crackers or little sandwiches with unidentifiable fillings or dip that smells like fish); (3) Keeping a crowd—or even a small group—rapt for an entire evening

I've always had a complex about this, thinking that everyone else's house is decorated with more charm, their entertainment dazzles more, or they make food that's way cuter than anything I could ever dream up. Please understand: I love having a house full of people; I'd just feel better about it if somebody with some taste did all the work.

Alas, this has never happened and is not likely to ever happen...for me...or for most of us, for that matter.

I've been through this song and dance so many times, I feel qualified to make up a few guidelines for my similarly challenged soul mates. In fact, I've condensed them into three basic steps:

Three Simple Steps to Easy Entertaining for Domestic Disasters
(1) Use other people's food.
(2) Go after what you really want.
(3) Enjoy!

All these steps I employed in one of the most fun gatherings I've ever hostessed: the Tacky Party. This proved to be the least stressful way to entertain, since everything was necessarily tacky, and my very essence is tacky. Of course, the first thing I did was to ask all my guests to provide tacky food, since I just didn't feel up to it. The definition of "tacky" food can be regional; what is tacky in one part of the country might actually be considered tasteful in another part. In these parts, it seemed that tacky food included cake with a few pieces missing, an abundance of potted meat and Vienna sausages, slightly stale crackers, and a lot of aerosol cheese product. Fantastic! I searched the archives of my party supplies for an assortment of napkins for different holidays (a few were so old, they were a little yellow, but all the better to be tacky with) and tossed them onto the table. Of course, we ate off of plastic and Styrofoam and did not hesitate to "double dip" our chips.

The longer the evening went on, the more relaxed and tacky the guests themselves became. One couple came an hour early,

just to be tacky. One couple came an hour late just to be tacky. One couple brought their uninvited kids, which was really tacky. And the best thing about it was, it didn't matter. You could do no wrong at this party; there were no social gaffes, since the party itself was pretty much a social gaffe.

No one had to worry about what to wear. We invited people to come in tacky clothing, so they arrived in everything from their pajamas to formals with fanny packs to leisure suits (lots of polyester that night). I personally chose my favorite green T-shirt with a 1978 photo of Barry Manilow, big as life, on the front. Do you know how liberating it is to dress for the evening, trying not to look good?

We gave prizes for the tackiest clothing, and we didn't even have to worry about choosing something the recipients would like. We just pulled a few things from the attic that we'd gotten as wedding presents (no shortage of tacky, inappropriate stuff there) and unloaded those treasures onto the "winners."

And the entertainment for the evening was the tackiest thing of all: stupid games. I realize that some people abso-lutely abhor party games, but—guess what—I didn't have to worry about being sensitive to my guest's desires because I was trying to be tasteless! One of my favorite activities that night was the Spoon Relay: In this game, you divide up into two teams, each team in a line. You hand the first person in line a spoon with a ball of string attached to it, and then instruct each team member to put the spoon/string down their shirt, through their pants, and out their pants leg, then pass it on to the next team member to do the same until the whole team is "threaded" together. What you're hoping for here is that everybody on your team chose to wear loose clothing that night. Anyway, then when the last person gets the string through, you "unthread" the team. The first team to complete the task wins the game, but probably not a prize, since we are being tacky here.

We also indulged in another one of my all-time favorite games: 100 Questions. To play this, everyone sits in chairs that form a circle. The leader asks a question that requires a yes or no answer. If you, as a player, must answer yes, you move one chair to the right. If you must answer no, you stay in your seat. That way, if you must answer no to a question (and stay put), and the person to your left must answer yes to the same question (and move to the right), that person ends up in your lap. Sometimes, after a number of questions, many people end up in your lap. It is great, rollicking fun for people with hardy laps.

And just a little advice: Start off with boring questions, such as, "Are you female?" and "Is your toothpaste green?" This will dupe reluctant participants into thinking that the game is relatively nonthreatening. Once they are relaxed and enjoying themselves, you can throw in more pointed questions: for example, "Do your measurements total over 100?" and "Have you ever been arrested?"

Play a few dumb games like that in an evening, and people will either really loosen up and have fun with it, or they will go home early. Which is okay, since—well, you know. Fortunately at this party, everyone enjoyed the games so much we had to put a few pieces of furniture out in the front yard to make room for the fun. And to top off the festivities, we decided to go Christmas caroling to our neighbors' houses (it was April).

At the end of the evening, I collapsed on the couch, worn out—from having fun, not from playing hostess.

Which reminds me of one time when Jesus visited Mary and Martha's home. Although I doubt that she was organizing entertainment that involved playing around with the flatware, Mary was having a fabulous time enjoying the presence of Jesus. Martha, on the other hand, was in the kitchen fixing the hors d'oeuvres. Of course, somebody has to make preparations for the guests, and of course, you can probably sympathize with Martha, because in your world, that somebody is probably usually you.

But remember what Jesus said to poor overworked Martha? *"You are worried and upset about many things, but only one thing is needed. Mary has chosen what is better"* (Luke 10:41–42). Because Mary chose to invest her best energy in her relationship with their most honored Guest, I must believe that the Guest later left their home revitalized and heartened.

With that in mind, it's important to remember that, in the same way, when you invite people into your home to rejuvenate them for a while, you are doing the same for Jesus.

A Tacky Party may seem to you like a hideous way to spend an evening with friends, but that's okay; the point is to entertain in a manner that stresses you least and delights everyone most. It is not really important to entertain the way the books, magazines, or home and garden TV shows tell you to. Honor your own uniqueness when you entertain, and I guarantee that your enthusiasm will energize your guests long after they say good night.

TRY THIS *Do you want to entertain, but resist doing it because it's too much work or you feel inadequate? Does the thought of hosting a gathering excite you and exhaust you at the same time? Determine the reason you really want to have people over. Then write down your personal style, even if it includes no cooking and no cleaning. Next, brainstorm ways you could entertain and stay within the guidelines of your personal style—more or less, anyway. How could you ease or eliminate stressors?*

WONDERLAND

19

Y ou may not know it when it happens, because it often happens quietly, but one day you may notice that life seems…well… a little boring. Maybe a lot boring. Like something's missing that used to be there, but you're not quite sure what that something is.

Maybe you've lost your wonder.

It's easy to do, since often at this time of life we have been working the same job for a number of years, living in the same town, going to the same church, involved in the same routines of life. Not that sameness and predictability are always a negative. I must admit that one of the "sames" of Christmas intrigued me every year, and that was my brother's propensity for getting sick on

TRY SOMETHING NEW.

our way home from our cousins' house on Christmas night. All of us would pile into the car after a day of feasting and merry-making with the family, knowing that it was only a matter of time before we'd have to stop the car and let him throw up on the side of the road. I don't recall being frightened at this, just fascinated. How, I marveled, did his gag reflex know it was Christmas night, year after year?

Rare, fascinating *sames* aside, consider whether you've mis-placed your fascination with life...the kind that comes from newness, from *first times*. The first time I rode a two-wheeled bike by myself, I was filled with wonder at my own mastery of the skill. The first time I saw the ocean, I was mesmerized and awed. The first time I went to Disney World, I thought I'd ecstatically entered another universe—the Land of the Terminally Cheerful. The first time Ben made a truly roman-tic gesture toward me, I was thrilled and excited to be in the "new discoveries" part of our relationship. He was a man of sur-prises—which I first found out as we were riding in the car on a long trip with several other people. As we drove back home in the dark, I could tell he had something he wanted to say to me, but four other people were in the car, and he didn't want them to hear. So he took my hand (easy enough to do, since I was glued to his side in the front seat) and started to draw letters on my palm. It didn't take long for me to understand that he was spelling out "I love you"—quite possibly the most romantic gesture anyone could ever dream up, in my opinion. Then, very tenderly, he picked up my hand and brought it to his face. I thought I would melt into a puddle right there, in anticipation of his next move....

And gently, with my index finger, he started picking his nose.

I shrieked, woke up everybody in the car, and knew that such a creative, albeit sick, man was born to be mine forever.

It's difficult, however, to maintain such red-hot fever for a very long time. You know how it goes: life gets in the way, we get busy, we get familiar, we get annoyed, and eventually even the wonder of picking your husband's nose gets old.

You long for moments when you honestly believe that if not another good thing ever happened to you it would be just fine, because you feel so full of the awe and mystery and excitement of discovery; you long for the wonder of first times.

These are the moments that may be a distant memory to your soul right now...but they don't have to be.

Once upon a time, I was feeling rather stale, in need of some of this freshness, and became convinced that one way to rediscover the wonder of the life God had given me was to inject a little novelty into it. My venture into newness, I decided, should probably be something small and simple—like downhill skiing. I had always wanted to learn, and though I was afraid that I might be too elderly, I nervously signed up for a ski trip anyway.

I rode the bus to Snow Land, rented the skis, and took the beginner lessons. Here they taught us one method of stopping: the snowplow, when you point your feet inward till your ski tips touch and form a wedge shape. "Cool," I thought. "Sounds like an easy way to control my speed. I'll be swooshing in no time." Of course, being a nonathlete, I took quite a few spills at first, but after a few hours, I was snowplowing my way down the bunny slopes without breaking anything. When I'd had enough for the day, I made my way over to a wide expanse of snow, where all the trails converged and led to the lodge. It was pretty high up, but I figured I could snowplow my way down and be okay.

Big mistake. I do not recall anyone telling me that you cannot, you must not, try to snowplow down a steep hill. But I didn't know any better, so down I went. At first it was okay, but as I picked up speed, I could see that this technique was going to be ineffective at best, and lethal at worst, because at the bottom of the hill were five hundred people, or so it seemed, milling around, waiting in lift lines, partying down. Little did they know just how down that party was about to be.

I tried snowplowing harder, but my legs just kept spreading farther and farther apart, until I couldn't even fall over. I could only keep going, faster and faster.

I tried yelling something like, "Comin' atcha!" or "Geronimo!" or "Fire!"—although it's hard to remember exactly what I screamed, because none of my warnings succeeded in parting the multitude. I was terrified, thinking that this must be what it feels like to run into an oncoming train.

And then I hit them, full force, my already-spread-apart legs spreading even farther. Can you say, "Wishbone"?

My body parts became their body parts in a painful, chaotic tangle of humans and skis. I also heard a few choice words aimed at describing my athletic ability and aptitude.

Miraculously, no one was seriously hurt. And I went on that day to take another ski lesson. By the end of the weekend, I could navigate that hill just fine, and I was filled with the exhilaration that comes from learning something new.

But that's not all—not even the most important part. To my surprise, the wonder came from the weekend as a whole, not just from trying to learn how to ski. It came from riding the ski lift one bright blue morning and seeing the sun shining through ice-covered trees. It came from camaraderie in a hot tub (see "Glamour Shots"). It came from laughing at some guys who tested the extreme air temperatures one night by running back to the lodge holding their swim trunks in front of them to see how long it would take them to freeze (answer: 32 seconds).

It also came as we stood together in front of a big fire, trying to thaw out. After about ten minutes, somebody sniffed the air and said, "Eww...what's that smell?" Somebody else said, "I don't know...but it's coming from Jill!" I thought they were joking, but realized they were quite right when I turned around, put my hand on my backside, and found that the fire was melting my snowsuit!

A little dismayed, not only because my derriere was sticking out far enough to catch fire, but also because no one else's was, I nevertheless had to laugh.

We also prayed for one another that weekend, worshipped together, and thanked God for bodies that were still generally in one piece when it was all over. I came back from the trip full of wonder—all because of a desire to try something new.

When was the last time you did something for the first time?

If it's been awhile, and you've been feeling less than wonder-*full* lately; if you're stuck in the muck of same ol' same ol' and long for someone to pick you up from here and set you down somewhere more exciting; if you just can't remember the last time you discovered something and were actually happy about it; then consider asking God to show you the wonder only He can stir up—the kind David celebrates as he says:

> He lifted me out of the slimy pit,
>   out of the mud and mire;
> he set my feet on a rock
>   and gave me a firm place to stand.
> He put a new song in my mouth,
>   a hymn of praise to our God.
> —Psalm 40:2–3

He may lead you someplace quiet; He may lead you snowplow-ing into a crowd of people. One thing's for sure: He will most certainly lead you into wonder.

TRY THIS *Make a list of moments/times in your life that were full of wonder. What do they have in common? Often, it's newness. Then answer this question: When was the last time you did something for the first time? Do something new this week, whether it involves cooking something new, wearing something new, or challenging your body or mind in a fun, new way.*

CHIMP

20

TAKE ADVANTAGE OF FLEETING MOMENTS TO PLAY.

Her name was Tootsie. She was a chimpanzee at the state fair, and for five dollars you could have a high-quality Instamatic photo taken with her. My mom and I happened to walk by, and when I caught sight of Tootsie and that irresistible offer, I begged, "Mom, Mom, please can we have our picture taken with the chimp? Pleeeeease?" But my mother resisted.

"Aw, come on, Mom. It'll be fun. Just this once?" I whined.

Still she declined.

"But why not?" I wanted to know.

"Well," she said slowly, obviously trying to think of a good reason, "20 years from now someone might get a look at it and think it was a three-generation picture."

Quick thinking on her part, and not a bad excuse. Still I was disappointed.

Keep in mind that I was 34 years old at the time, and my mother was 70. I had my own money, and I could have gotten my own picture taken with the ape, thank you very much. But I respectfully caved in, even though I just knew that someday my mom would look back with angst and regret at having passed up that little moment of whimsy.

I am usually pretty good with moments of whimsy, but at times, I, like most of us, am also pretty good at letting fleeting opportunities to play just continue to fleet on by. This pertains to just about anything a child (even a 34-year-old child!) might want you to do. During a summer shower once, my daughter Jamie begged me to put on a bathing suit with her and walk around the neighborhood with an umbrella. I actually said no first; I mean, really, what would the neighbors think? Then I thought, "Who cares? How many more chances in this life will I have to parade around the neighborhood in my bathing suit in the rain under an umbrella with my five-year-old?" So we did it. And no one reported us for indecent exposure or anything else. For just a little while, life just didn't get any better than that. Have I ever regretted catching that fleeting moment? No way.

My daddy was always a gifted "catcher." On one vacation when I was about eight years old, we went to Chicago. For some reason, my father and I had separated from my mom and my brother, so we were wandering around the Museum of Science and Industry by ourselves. True to form, I can't recall a single thing about that museum except one: the moment I spied one of those instant photo booths and begged my daddy to jump into the booth with me to have our picture taken in front of that cool background curtain. And true to *his* form, he was ready. We didn't worry about how we looked; we probably thought we were lookin' good. I had one great pixie haircut, with my bangs about a foot above my eyebrows; he was wearing a white shirt and a bow tie. (I don't know why.)

Now that tiny picture sits in a frame on my dresser, and I can't tell you how many times I have stared at it and thanked God for letting us take time captive for a moment. It was only two years later that he died very suddenly, way before it was time, and way before I was finished being his little girl.

That photo has been a constant reminder of how important it is to take advantage of fleeting moments…which is why I eventually went on a hunt to find a photogenic chimpanzee, and trick my mom into—I mean, give my mom another chance at—being in the photo of a lifetime. I was so serious about it that I put "find a chimp" on my prayer list. I am certain God was amused.

After searching for several years, I finally found one right here in Hanover County, Virginia. Curtis and Bea Shepperson have their own little zoo and a chimp that loves to interact with people. When I called and told them what I wanted to do, explaining that my mom and the rest of my family would be in town for my daughter's wedding, they even offered to bring the chimp to our house for an hour for the big surprise.

On Friday before the wedding, my extended family had arrived. I broke the news to Mom, telling her that I needed some closure on that traumatic loss of opportunity in my life, and that the chimp would be arriving at 10:30 A.M. She could run but she could not hide, I warned, so she might as well put some lipstick on and smile for the camera. She loved it!

Sierra arrived right on time. She was a little shy at first, but we found that if we held grapes and raisins, she would at least stay with us long enough to pose for some pictures. After a while, she relaxed a lot and let us play with her. Believe me when I say that you have not truly lived until you've invited a chimpanzee into your home for an hour or so of primal frolicking. She turned somersaults, leaped off chairs, "kissed" us when we had grapes in our mouths, let us scratch her belly, and jumped all over us. It was so much fun, in fact, it was a little scary since, by the end of the hour, we were all acting pretty much alike.

Anyway, a dream of mine was to have a family portrait made with the chimp amongst us, like one of the kids, so we all gathered around for a photo shoot. I would love to hear the comments from future generations as they pull out this picture from some dusty box somewhere.

"Who are these people, Mommy?" an unsuspecting child will someday ask.

"Oh," Mommy will say, "that's ol' Uncle Ben, the man who never would admit that the Civil War was over and his side lost. And there's crazy Uncle Ted; he was mayor of Bluffton, Indiana, for 44 years. And look at sweet Aunt Marge; she bravely sacrificed her own reputation to marry Uncle Ted. And there's wacky Aunt Jill; her mind was as loopy as her hair. And those beautiful young ones, cousins Andy, Nikki, Becky, Trey, little Curtis,…and Jamie and Keith, whose wedding that year was voted The Most Beautiful Wedding in the History of the World. Of course, there's Grandma Mary, who suffered for years from "primataphobia," poor thing…and…well, I'm not sure who that hairy baby is… some little mutation of the genes, probably…although she does resemble the rest of them in an odd way. Must be those nifty opposable thumbs…."

Just thinking about this contribution to posterity makes me smile. It was the icing on the cake of a wonderful weekend: we added a son-in-law *and* a primate to the family album. Closure, indeed.

Believe it or not, Jesus was my inspiration for arranging this little celebration. His first recorded miracle in John 2 shows how He took advantage of a fleeting moment at a wedding party. Everyone was having a fine time when, to the host's dismay, the wine ran out. (In Virginia, this is similar to the tragedy of running out of ham biscuits. When I first came South, I'd never even

heard of ham biscuits, but I soon learned that no one is married, buried, or invited to any special occasion when two or more people are gathered without ham biscuits. And if you run out of ham biscuits, you might as well send everybody home, because believe you me, they won't be staying.)

I can just imagine Jesus smiling to Himself as He told the servants to fill six stone jars with water, then draw some out and take it to the head honcho.

> Jesus said to the servants, "Fill the jars with water"; so they filled them to the brim.
>
> Then he told them, "Now draw some out and take it to the master of the banquet."
>
> They did so, and the master of the banquet tasted the water that had been turned into wine. He did not realize where it had come from, though the servants who had drawn the water knew. Then he called the bridegroom aside and said, "Everyone brings out the choice wine first and then the cheaper wine after the guests have had too much to drink; but you have saved the best till now."
> —John 2:7–10

I am certainly not putting our little escapade on par with the way Jesus demonstrated His power that day; however, I am inspired by His willingness to take advantage of a precious moment during a celebration and give the guests even more reason to celebrate.

That's why I believe, had He been in my family that day, Jesus would have been the first in line to jump into the photo with the chimp to preserve that fleeting moment of playfulness. He wants to remind all of us that this opportunity might not be here tomorrow or an hour from now or even five minutes from now...and God has actually *saved the best till now.*

TRY THIS

Have you ever passed up a fleeting opportunity for fun, only to regret it later? Make a note of it, and post it in a prominent place. Remember that one the next time you get a momentary chance to play, and catch the moment.

PLAY IN THE SAND

21

TAKE A VACATION... BUT NOT TO ESCAPE!

Next time you're in a roomful of people, shout, "Hey, anybody got a vacation disaster story?" You'll be there all night swapping tales of woe. I promise. This is not to say that vacations are bad—I love them—only that the best way to get ready for one is to (*a*) live the rest of your mundane life pretending that you're on one, and (*b*) avoid thinking that you're on vacation to escape reality.

Let me explain: (*a*) Haven't you noticed that when you're on vacation, you wake up most days in a state of anticipation, looking forward to the day and its promises of delight? This is good; keep doing this. But (*b*) remember that if you can't play well in the moments and days of the rest of the year, my guess is you won't be very good at vacation.

The idea of taking a vacation to escape reality is, in my opinion, not only overrated, but also dangerous, mainly because…well…what if it all goes wrong? Or even a little something goes wrong? If you've seen the movie *City Slickers*, you'll remember the three middle-aged guys on a quest to escape from their *real lives* that were full of what most real lives are full of: jobs, financial burdens, and family responsibilities, with a lot of ordinariness thrown in on the side. They had done everything from Baseball Fantasy Camp to running with the bulls in Pamplona, and were now getting ready for their greatest escape of all: a Western cattle drive. Of course, disaster strikes, and they end up finding out that life's meaning is not found in escaping life. Can I get a witness to that?

I'll bet I can—from everyone who has ever tried to make a break for it by taking a vacation that turned out to be less than the thrilling adventure they envisioned.

Cruises—while many people think they are fantastic—seem to be ripe environments for surprises. Our friends Wayne and Jeanne took a cruise. They packed warm-weather clothes, dreamed of tropical beaches, and got on a boat to paradise. But it just so happened, their boat was the last one to leave the port before it closed. A big storm was brewing. It was a good thing they didn't know it. Well, they didn't know it until 20-foot waves started pitching their boat around. Most of the guests spent the next couple of days hurling into the Atlantic.

At least they had paradise to look forward to…but paradise turned out to be a lot colder than they anticipated. Freak weather. It almost never happened, claimed the natives. Jeanne brought only one pair of long pants. She wore them four days in a row.

Actually, planning an escape that depends on the weather is asking for trouble. What do you do when you go to the beach

and it rains all week? ("Fight and eat," said a friend of mine who returned from six straight days of downpours. Of course, it cleared up as they were leaving.)

Most likely, though, we violate the true meaning of a vacation when we orchestrate and engineer the good time right on out of a good time. Our first trip to Disney World was a great example of this. Ben and I, as young parents, were set to give our daughter Jamie, then six years old, a few days of relentless fun. We stayed off the Disney property, so every morning we had to get up at 6:00 in order to get breakfast at 7:00 and be panting at the gates when they opened at 8:00, so we could race around the park till it closed. We never got around to dinner until about 9:00 each evening, but that was the time when we could talk about all the fun we'd had that day...right before we fell face down into our plates...asleep.

On the third day, we were on Paradise Island, waiting for a ferry to take us back to the Magic Kingdom for more fun. Jamie was having a fine time playing in the sand when the boat arrived. "Come on, honey," we urged. Time to go somewhere else!"

"But I don't *want* to go somewhere else! I want to play in the sannnnnd."

"No, sweetie, we don't have *time* to play in the sand. We need to go fly out of Wendy's window with Peter Pan, and go through 'It's a Small World' for the nineteenth time, and watch Dumbo's ears grow for awhile. Remember, we're leaving tomorrow, and we need to cram all the outrageous fun we can into the teeny amount of time we have left. Come onnnnnnnn."

She protested. She cried. We took her on the ferry anyway.

Then day number four dawned. On the monorail by 8:00 A.M., Ben and I were wide-eyed and ready for another day, our last day, and were happily telling Jamie what a good time she was having.

"Isn't this exciting, honey? Oh look! See the bushes shaped like animals? And over there! There's Mickey Mouse! And look!

Cinderella's Castle from yet a different angle! Oh, honey, isn't this great? Aren't we having fun?"

To which she replied, "I wanna go to bed."

Oops.

Jim Molnar, writing for *The Seattle Times*, warns us about trying to engineer a true escape: "So what about our vacations, when we head into artificial environments set up to produce calculated experiences and evoke standardized responses? Perfect beaches, perfect trees, perfect flowers, organized activities—different from but every bit as predictable as the routines we're on holiday from. No worries.

"I suppose there's some fun in trading one unreality for another, but…traveling properly is an escape into reality…. *It's seeing all there is to see, not just what we're supposed to look at.*"

A great vacation is not about escape or avoidance. It's all about tapping the joy that already sits deep inside every one of us, just waiting to surface, whether in a burst of enthusiasm or a quiet, blissed-out attitude. In other words, if you are delighting in playing in the sand, and some well-meaning but clueless traveling companion says, "Time to go and have fun," you can calmly explain to them that what you are doing *is* the fun, and they probably need to practice listening to their "funsense" at home so that they will be willing to let it surface while they are away from home.

So even if your vacation takes a couple of unexpected turns for the worse, you'll have a willingness to let delight surface at any unexpected, unscheduled moment that may not have made the agenda. You may use my friends Bob and Nancy as your inspiration. They had driven to Yosemite from Virginia in June and were expecting some degree of warmth, since Virginia is warm in June. *Big mistake*, they learned, as they lay in their sleeping bags one night, shivering in subfreezing temperatures. Of course, as any good outdoorsman (or outdoors *woman*) knows, you lose a lot of heat from your head, so to stay warm they

searched for covering. Having no wool hats, they found a perfect solution. Well, Bob found the solution, and really it wasn't
exactly perfect, since his kids threatened to leave the family if
he *ever* told *anybody* that he had them all spending the night with
their underwear on their heads. But it did make for some light-
heartedness (not to mention warmth) in a disappointing turn
of events.

The prophet Habakkuk spoke to a group of people who
had more serious problems than vacation disasters: Judah was
facing devastation in the form of crop failure and the death of
animals; however, Habakkuk encouraged them to focus on God
and not their difficulties:

> *Though the fig tree does not bud*
> *and there are no grapes on the vines,*
> *though the olive crop fails*
> *and the fields produce no food,*
> *though there are no sheep in the pen*
> *and no cattle in the stalls,*
> *yet I will rejoice in the* LORD,
> *I will be joyful in God my Savior.*
> —Habakkuk 3:17–18

Remember his words when you encounter a less-than-idyllic
time on vacation...or in life...and insert your own troubles, big
or small, into this Scripture as I have:

> Though it rains all week at the beach
> and everyone is bummed;
> though the waves are fifty feet high around this cruise ship
> and thousands are throwing up into a vast
> undulating sea,
> though we get lost, have flat tires,
> and encounter bad food and crummy accommodations,

yet I will rejoice in the LORD,
    I will be joyful in God my Savior,
because, no matter what happens, I can tap into the
    True Source of joy
    and escape into that reality.

TRY THIS *Okay, go ahead. Tell your vacation disaster story. In fact, get a group of people together for that very purpose. How did you respond? If your response was not mature, positive, and joyful (if you were childish, negative, and cranky), how could a positive response have changed the atmosphere? Talking about vacation disasters is a lot of fun. And remember, if your next vacation goes south, you should be practiced up on having daily fun, so it doesn't feel like a total loss. Take Habakkuk: 3:17–18 with you and insert your own challenges, just to maintain perspective.*

STORIES FROM

MIDDLE ADULTHOOD

COW SUIT

22

DRAW FROM THE JOY.

My husband and I have dealt with infertility for most of our married life. God gave us one beautiful daughter, Jamie, and we enjoyed her so much that for 20 years we asked for more children. He didn't lead us to adopt; physically, we weren't candidates for other methods of conception; and now, at this point in my life, God has to take me by the shoulders and say: "Look at me. No more, I say—no more babies." And for a very long time, I felt profoundly sad. Getting up in the morning was really hard; facing the day and everything I was supposed to be doing was really hard. Often I just wanted to curl up with a blanket over my head and wait for life to go away.

When a dream dies or life just doesn't turn out like you planned, finding joy can be a challenge.

But God came to my rescue in the form of a cow.

We had a basketball banquet at our church; it was catered by Chick-fil-A, a restaurant that does chicken in a most wonderful way. As part of the entertainment, the Chick-fil-A cow came bopping in, mingled with the kids, and gave out prizes. I was instantly intrigued.

I looked at Ben and said, "I could do that."

He said, "Why don't you?"

I laughed.

A few weeks later we were eating in our local Chick-fil-A, and Jamie urged me to talk to the manager.

"What qualifications does a person have to have to get in that furry suit and be the cow?" I asked.

"A pulse," he said.

So I got an application, and a few days later, the market representative called and asked if I could meet her for an interview. Really excited and anxious to have a little fun, I pulled together my college transcripts, a resume, and some references and met her at the mall. We talked, and after a few minutes, ever the professional, she shook my hand and said, "I am delighted to offer you this position as the Area Market Cow for Chick-fil-A." My, I felt as if I'd just been elected president... of *something*.

My first gig was a couple weeks later at the mall.

I met her in the catacombs behind the food court, ready to hop into that suit and charm my way into the hearts of unsuspecting shoppers.

If you have never been in a cow suit, I must tell you that those duds are HOT. Climbing into the furry body, I laughed and said, "Wow, just like wearing toasty winter jammies!" Next, I slid my feet into the big hooves and said, "Wow, just like wearing big winter boots in the snow!" Then she put the gloves on my hands, and I said, "Wow, just like warm, woolly winter mittens!" I was actually breaking quite a sweat by this time, but the biggest challenge was yet to come: the head. When she plopped that huge thing on top of my shoulders, my mere sweat turned into a racing heart. I could see nothing except my feet. The only place to see out was the cow's mouth, and, by golly, it was *dark* in there! I couldn't scratch my nose; I couldn't wipe the sweat out of my eyes! I couldn't see! I couldn't breathe! The temperature shot up about 20 degrees, I went completely claustrophobic, and I was about to yell "GET ME OUTTA HERE!"

I stopped short of ripping the head off and running out into the parking lot, because I thought, "You can't do that. You've told everyone you know that you're going to be this cow. You've got what it takes, girl; now just get out there and do it!" I felt like one of those guys I once saw on a TV show about Navy SEAL training…only there was more at stake here.

Fortunately, my little pep talk worked; I eventually relaxed enough to venture out into the mall and actually had a great time.

I didn't truly realize what was happening on a deeper level though, until exactly one year after I first saw the cow; it was the night of the basketball awards banquet, and this year I was wearing the suit. As I was standing behind a door, waiting for my turn to go on, I could feel God's reminder that yes, He really meant it when He said I was to have no more babies: I could feel the hormonal furnace revving up inside me, the temperature in that suit rising fast, and I thought, "What a perfect picture of joy and sadness together—me having a hot flash in a cow suit."

I had to laugh, and in that moment, God reminded me that it is possible to nurture a playful spirit even in a hard place.

For the longest time, I had perceived myself as an obsessively upbeat, positive, happy girl. Then losses came, one after another, and one day I couldn't figure out whether I was basically still a happy girl with a lot of sadness or now a very sad person with a few good times thrown in on the side. It turns out that I, like most of us, am neither…and both.

To be sure, sorrow shouldn't be denied, but neither should it be our address. It just becomes a part of who we are. To deny that is to deny God the chance to work in our lives—through the loss and because of the loss—and bring us to a place where we can not only empathize with and encourage others, but also find comfort and encouragement ourselves, knowing that joy and sorrow can indeed walk hand in hand through the same life.

Isaiah, as all prophets in the Bible, had a tough job that included a lot of "Well, people, I've got some good news…and some bad news…." The bad news, I'm sure, was just as hard for him to give as it was for the nation of Judah to receive. Fortunately, though, there were times when it was followed by a message of hope. Always a personal favorite of mine is this passage from Isaiah 61:

> The Spirit of the Sovereign LORD is on me,
>> because the LORD has anointed me to preach good news to the poor.
> He has sent me to bind up the brokenhearted,
>> to proclaim freedom for the captives…
> to comfort all who mourn,
> and to provide for those who grieve."
> —Isaiah 61:1–3a

Ah, that must have felt good indeed…just like a message of hope feels good to you indeed.

And here is one such message: The Spirit of the Sovereign Lord is on you, too, if you know Him. This means that you, too, have been asked by God to preach good news, to bind up the brokenhearted, to comfort all who mourn, and to give those who are depressed, including yourself at times, some really good stuff:

The oil of gladness
*   instead of mourning,*
and a garment of praise
*   instead of a spirit of despair.*
—Isaiah 61:3*b*

TRY THIS

Where is your sorrow these days? What are the joys in your life that might walk alongside that sorrow? Write down both, and keep the lists. Add to them both, but be sure to keep them side by side and make an effort to draw from the joy, even in the middle of the sadness.

PIGSKIN

23

D on't you ever marvel at people who do things that you would never do? For instance, I am in awe of anyone who could find it in themselves to jump out of an airplane. I just can't see myself being this brave—even with a parachute; even piggyback on someone who supposedly has done this before and knows what they are doing; even with the prospect of getting my picture taken as I free-fall from a billion feet above sea level, doing this thing so daring and so cool that I just know would impress beyond measure everyone on earth. But personally, I *would* like to *have been* skydiving.

It's the same with caving. It seems like such adventure to "spelunk" your way through the belly of the earth, crawling

LEARN
ABOUT A
FRIEND'S FUN.

around on your stomach, with mere inches between the top of your head and the ceiling of the cave; such adventure to find yourself squeezing though tight spaces in the dark, knowing that there's nothing between you and eternal blackness but a few batteries; such adventure to creep around in damp, bat-filled spaces, knee deep in guano…. Well, as is the case with skydiving, it's something I'd like to say I did *last year.*

There are also fun things other people do that we don't really fear—we're just not exactly driven to try them. We might be missing something here, though, when we don't make the effort to stretch a little and actually *share* in what our friends are doing. Often I have found unexpected exhilaration in the uncharted territory of a buddy's good time.

Let me explain. My husband is a huge fan of college football—Virginia Tech football in particular. For years, I have been one of those people who sat on the sidelines, mystified by the appeal this sport has for my husband; I've also felt pretty guilty about interrupting his concentration by asking question after question, since I never have understood the details of it. I've always known the "First and ten! Do it again!" cheer from high school, but it has always seemed to me to be a game where (*a*) you can never tell where the ball really is. The play starts, and it just looks like a bunch of guys all squooshing together on the field, and (*b*) the clock stops every five seconds, which I find highly annoying. Anyway, I'd been meaning to learn more about football some day, and I got my chance when Ben gave me my Christmas present last year: a reservation in Coach Frank Beamer's Football Clinic for Ladies. Yes, believe it or not, hundreds of women actually pay for a day at Virginia Tech to learn about playing with pigskin.

I was really looking forward to a sort of "Football for Dummies" day. The first couple of sessions, however, were obviously for women who knew the game, since they were demonstrating the finer points of particular plays. Being ignorant of the basics, though, I was drowning in a sea of sport-specific terminology.

When these big, beefy men started tossing around phrases like, "push the pocket," "stick and rip," "outside hand knockdown skate rush," and "horizontal stretch on the defensive coverage," I wanted to raise my hand and ask where the remedial students were supposed to be. On and on they went about "perpetrators," "ventilators," "agitators," and (I think) "defibrillators." At one point, I did perk up a bit when I heard "tight ends," but then got lost again in "back ends," "side ends," "split ends," and "rear ends," or something like that. I can't remember now.

What I was hoping to learn, in addition to the basics of the game, was sort of a behind-the-scenes, "unplugged" version of football—an insider's look at the life of a football player. What do they eat? How do they cope with the pressure? What goes on in the locker room after a big loss? …after a big win? …in the middle of the game? What all are they wearing under those jerseys? What kinds of mind games do they play with themselves and other players? I would especially like to know more about intimidation. For instance, when these guys are head to head, waiting for the snap, what are they *really* saying to the guys on the other team about their mothers?

Alas, my questions were never answered. But it was a fun day anyway, learning more about my husband's favorite sport. In fact, the best part came at the end when we were allowed to walk through the weight room, into the tunnel, and out onto the field. We took a bunch of pictures: first Ben hanging around the goalpost, then me hanging around the goalpost, then me on Ben's shoulders hanging onto the goalpost for dear life. And even though I was still pretty much a football dummy at that point, I was looking back on the day and calling it a rousing success. After all, I got to spend time with a loved one and add another shared memory to our relationship. That, to me, was more important than any activity either of us could dream up.

I can imagine people in the early Christian church trying out each other's fun, too, mainly because:

All the believers were together and had everything in common.
Selling their possessions and goods, they gave to anyone as he had
need. Every day they continued to meet together in the temple courts.
They broke bread in their homes and ate together with glad and
sincere hearts, praising God and enjoying the favor of all the people.
—Acts 2:44–47

Just imagine: they shared everything—from their homes and possessions to their food and their faith; they were heavily involved in the others' lives. As a result, I can also imagine them sharing their heartaches and their recreation with one another—something we do all too seldom for lack of time or energy. I would encourage you to make a little time and muster up a little energy to learn about—even engage in—the fun of a friend. You never know when, as a result, God will lay a little bonus on you.

After we had exhausted ourselves posing for goalpost pictures and were getting ready to head home from football camp, I stopped one last time to appreciate the magnificent perspective we had, looking up into those expansive stands from down on the turf. And then I was seized by an irresistible urge.

"Ben," I said. "Can you wait just a minute? I really want to run to the other end of the field."

I'm sure he felt like rolling his eyes, but he indulged me by saying, "Sure. Go for it."

And I tore off (well, trotted off), running the entire length of the football field and back, with my hands in the air, acknowledging the imaginary roaring crowd. It was fabulous. I really did feel like—and Ben says I actually looked like—an official "rear end."

Oh, the satisfaction of a day well played.

Maybe you won't end up falling in love with another person's sport or scrapbooking or clogging or painting, but I can guarantee that your friendship and even your life will be at least a little bit richer for the sharing. Go for it.

TRY THIS

Do you have a friend who has fun in a way you've never tried? Don't wait for an invitation; ask her to introduce you to something new, and give it your best shot. Or take the reverse approach: invite a friend to share in your kind of fun.

RISKY BUSINESS

24

**TAKE A
RISK!**

Many people—and maybe you're one of them—fancy themselves as adventurous risk takers. Unfortunately most of us are really chickens at heart, a little bit (or a lot) afraid of risks.

However, sometimes I am willing to take a risk just to get the feeling of having taken one (unless the risk is skydiving or spelunking; see "Pigskin").

Such was the case when I signed up for a program sponsored by our Department of Game and Inland Fisheries called Becoming an Outdoors Woman in Virginia. It was a weekend full of classes ranging from canoeing to pistol shooting, and I was convinced that it was time for me to add some excitement to my life by trying something a little risky.

In anticipation of this event, I found it easy to drum up the excitement, with a dash of fear and trepidation thrown in.

I arrived, ready to register for some canoeing and outdoor cooking, but was most intrigued by the description of the high ropes course: a series of wire configurations that you have to navigate about 30 feet off the ground. I could imagine myself having done this stunt and feeling like quite the brave one, so I signed up. I expected more problem solving than risky behavior. I mean, how dangerous could it be, with all these people doing it? Besides, I'd heard of eight-year-old kids tackling *low* ropes courses, and what was a *high* ropes course but a low ropes course higher off the ground?

I was actually looking forward to the experience until just a few hours before the class, when I talked to a girl about 20 years younger than me who had done it the year before. "Oh wow!" she practically shouted at me. "You'll love it! I had bruises all over my body, but it was awesome! You'll be so proud of yourself when it's all over! When you're up there, just keep repeating to yourself, 'Nothing's gonna happen to me, nothing's gonna happen to me.'" This was obviously more than I had bargained for. That afternoon we met as a group and walked to the woods where the high ropes were…very high ropes. I never knew 30 feet off the ground could look so high. Greg, our instructor, showed us how to hitch ourselves into harnesses and onto hooks called carabiners, and then he let us practice a few safety techniques.

After an hour of instruction, we assembled at the bottom of the first station. I did not volunteer to go first. I preferred to let my anxiety build while I watched other people brave the unknown. The first girl got around the course (four configurations) slowly and haltingly, but at least she made it, as did most other people. The closer my turn got, the harder my heart pounded. I wasn't too afraid of heights or even of getting hurt. I was just afraid that I couldn't do this thing—that I would fail and be what I most dreaded being in this life: a weenie.

As I hooked up my belay line to a lady I did not know and who had never held someone's life in her hands before, I worried that I didn't have the muscle strength or the balance to make the climb to get to the wires. The steps were two feet apart, and when I got to the top step, I had to get on my knees and hoist myself up to the platform. I stood up, shaking and out of breath.

The first challenge was a single wire to walk on and two wires to hold on to about shoulder height. I wobbled and swayed my way across. (They really should pull those things tighter.) Feeling all alone in this world, I continued on. I made it to the second platform and contemplated the second station: the kitten crawl across two parallel wires. I was supposed to lower myself slowly to my hands and knees, walk my hands out on the wires and pray that my legs were following behind me—knees inside the wires, feet outside. At this point, all my confidence left me; I wanted to leap off the platform and run home.

But there was nothing to do except keep going, so I got down on all fours, slowly, slowly…and started scooting, my knees waggling in and out, in and out. Halfway across, I was panting, cotton mouthed, and wondering why I did these things to myself; the end of the line looked a mile away, and my knees were moving in and out just a tad too much when—shoot! I flipped off the wires and, in an instant, found myself hanging upside down, suspended in the air from my belay line. And it was at this moment—gazing up at the blinding sun—that I recalled what Greg had told us from the beginning: "It's not important to be the best; it's not even important to be good. What's important is to be here."

Yes, indeedy. And here I was, hanging upside down like a sloth in a tree.

I had a little talk with Jesus right then and there. Certainly this was a good time to thank Him for the wires and hooks that kept me from plummeting to the ground. I was also moved to ask Him for help in getting out of this awkward—not to mention unnatural—position. He told me to look to my friends.

"NOW WHAT?" I yelled at everyone below, suddenly aware that I had an audience.

"GET BACK ON TOP!" they yelled.

Right, I thought. *Part the Red Sea! Walk on water! Get back on top! It's all the same to me.*

"HOW?" I yelled back down.

Well, their instructions didn't help much, and I ended up pulling myself across, still inverted, with my arms. Finally, I made it to the platform, too weak to right myself, and Greg gave me a hand up.

The next two configurations were easy in comparison, but I passed through them with shaky legs, flimsy knees, and a badly bruised ego. A reward was waiting for me, however, at the last station: the zip line. I was on a platform up in a tree. A wire extended from high up in that tree and descended into the woods about a quarter mile away. I was delighted to see that there was no challenge to this challenge: it was like swinging through the jungle on a vine. Greg hooked me up to the line and said, "Okay, jump when you're ready"—and I had absolutely no problem leaping off that platform and sailing down into the woods with a Tarzan yodel and wild abandon.

Was the risk (and reality) of failure and bruises worth the payoff at the end? Oh my, yes!

Would I do it all again? Absolutely...because the most valuable lesson I learned from having taken this risk was that if I fail—or even just look like a sloth in a tree—the exhilaration of having stepped out on the wire to get to the reward is far more fun than standing on the ground wishing I had the nerve to play Tarzan.

Some of the "risks" God calls us to take are far more serious than this one. Even a mere glance at Hebrews 11 will show you that.

"By faith, Noah built a ship in the middle of dry land" (Hebrews 11:7 *The Message*), risking his reputation as a man with an operating brain.

"By an act of faith, Abraham said yes to God's call to travel to an unknown place that would become his home. When he left he had no idea where he was going" (Hebrews 11:8 *The Message*), which might not seem risky to

those of us who are directionally impaired and experience this regularly, but to a man leading his family, which the Lord had promised would become a great nation—verrrry perilous.

"By an act of faith, Moses' parents hid him away for three months after his birth" (Hebrews 11:23 The Message) in direct opposition to a king's decree. Now that was a major risk!

"By an act of faith, Israel walked through the Red Sea on dry ground"— really risky, because right afterward, *"The Egyptians tried it and drowned"* (Hebrews 11:29 The Message).

The difference, of course, between these people and others who are simply thrill seekers is this: each of their risks was an act of faith, a response to God's voice, a result of their trust in Him.

Couldn't the same principle apply to adventures He might nudge you toward, even when it comes to having fun? I believe we take playful risks far too infrequently and, as a result, miss out on much of the ordinary joy God intends for us to experience. Surely He has zip lines waiting for you in even the most mundane of days, if only you'll be willing to maybe wobble a bit, just to get the chance to jump out of your tree and yodel with wild abandon.

TRY THIS *Is there a risk you've been wanting to take? …a risk that God has been wanting you to take? Write it down, put it on your prayer list, and list the reasons you haven't taken it yet. Risks run the gamut from speaking in public to changing careers to going on a trip to some faraway place when you are prone to seasickness or afraid of flying. Whatever the risk, take it at God's next nudge.*

RIDE ON

25

Y ou may or may not be a list
maker. If you're not, you probably bristle at the thought of
being confined to a few items on
a piece of paper that supposedly dictate
the events of your day, or maybe you
just have a superhuman memory.
Some people, however, are married
to their lists. My husband, Ben, always
has a running to-do list on whatever's
handy—a napkin, an index card, a piece
of paper bag—and he is *never* without the
list, both on paper and in his mind. In
fact, I used to complain about the nature
of his calls when he would phone me
from a business trip. Since he usually
had been gone at least a couple of days,
I would expect a few sweet nothings, an
"I miss you and can hardly breathe without

MAKE
A LIST.

you" kind of conversation. However, most often he would greet me, and then start off a series of what I call "didjas": "Didja get the mail yet?" "Didja take the dog to the vet?" "Didja pick up the dry cleaning?"

It used to drive me crazy, because no matter how smooth he was trying to be, I could tell that our whole exchange was driven by that doggone list of his; I knew he was looking right at it, checking items off as I said yes, rather than thinking of more sweet nothings to murmur into the phone. However, I have since accepted and even come to embrace his list making; that man can get more done in a day than I can in a week, and all because he eats and sleeps with his little list.

There is another type list, however, that even non–list makers can embrace, and that is the Fun Stuff I Want to Do Before I Die list. (Variations of that list include the Fun Stuff I Want to Do This Summer, Fun Stuff I Want to Do This Month, and Fun Stuff I Want to Do at Work lists—you get the idea.) The concept is this: there's something about the act of writing down your thoughts that tucks ideas into your brain and alerts your subconscious to opportunities or actions you can take to make these things happen. I am certain some scientist some-where has proven this with a study; more importantly, though, I believe God sometimes chooses to work through our lists (much as I hate to admit this to Ben).

Here's how to start: Right now, stop reading and brainstorm a list of all the fun things you'd like to do before you leave this earth. Do not be limited by money or reason; just barrel ahead and write down anything and everything. And when you think you're out of ideas, keep going anyway. You'll probably find more that have been gathering dust in the back of your mind for a while. Keep the list where you can see it, and add to it as you think of more things.

A word of caution here: all you task-oriented people must resist the temptation to drift into adding work-related items, household chores, and career and ministry goals in this exercise. Put those somewhere else and reserve this for pure fun.

As of today, I have 53 items on my list. Some I have actually done, such as hike the Grand Canyon; many more, however, are still rumbling around in my spirit. Some would seem out of reach unless God Himself does some heavy intervening ("get a personal invitation to eat dinner with the President at the White House"); some would seem as simple as doing the research and making a trip ("swim with dolphins"); some appear challenging but doable ("learn to salsa"—okay, maybe God would have to intervene to make that happen); some are just silly, but I want to do them anyway ("sing 'Danke Schoen' at a karaoke place where nobody knows me"). All of them I hope to do someday, and along the way, I hope I can help others to do the same...as I once did for my friend Sue.

Several years ago, she told me that one thing she wanted to do someday was to ride a Harley—just to feel the wind in her face, hear the "potato-potato-potato" rumble of the engine in her ears, and experience the power of the ultimate "hog." Not knowing anyone who owned one, she filed that little wish away on her To Do Someday list and went on with the business of life.

As her 50th birthday approached, I wanted to give her something special, and remembered her Harley dream from a few years before. "Perfect," I thought, as I searched for and ultimately found John—a willing Harley guy.

Unaware of my plans, Sue and her husband Ron came to our house for a visit. About 15 minutes after she arrived, John roared up our street as I cranked up the stereo to play "Born to Be Wild"; he stopped in front of the house, hopped off his Harley, strode up to the door, and rang the doorbell. I introduced him to Sue and said, "Here's your birthday present, girl. Jump on the bike and have the ride of your life!"

She nearly fainted with delight when she caught sight of that Harley. Then she laughed, she screamed, and she almost

cried. I have never seen anyone so excited in my life as she was when John fixed her helmet and she threw her leg over the side of that bike.

Anyway, as they roared off into the sunset, she flung her arms out and yelled, "Woohooooooo!" and away they went on a cloud of exhaust and adventure.

It was a picture I will always hold in my heart as proof that, even though our joyfulness may seem dormant as we get older, we should bring it out to play often.

Keeping a Fun Stuff I Want to Do list is not a new idea, and many people find the concept appealing. Few, however, actually put it into action, often because their "play muscles" are way out of shape, or they feel guilty spending time and energy on something they believe is so frivolous. But we mustn't forget about the freedom of the mind and spirit we are privileged to experience just by virtue of the fact that God is watching over us. I love Moses's description of that liberation in Deuteronomy 32 when he talks about how God had protected Israel:

> *In a desert land he found him,*
> *in a barren and howling waste.* [Can you relate?]
> *He shielded him and cared for him;*
> *he guarded him as the apple of his eye.*
> —Deuteronomy 32:10

Then he compares God's past care of the Israelites and His relationship with His people to *"an eagle that stirs up its nest and hovers over its young, that spreads its wings to catch them and carries them on its pinions"* (v. 11). And because of that leadership and protection, God *"made him ride the heights of the land"* (v. 13).

What a picture! Read that Scripture again, and imagine yourself without boundaries, mental or physical. Then consider this: if you first pray for God to guide your heart and mind as you pick up a pen and start a list, you will most certainly find yourself very close to riding the heights of the land of adventures you've only dreamed about until now.

TRY THIS

Is there something fun you've always wanted to do and just haven't gotten around to it yet for some reason? Start a list— a life list, a this year list, a summer list. And remember, put only fun things on it—nothing like "lose ten pounds" or "paint the kitchen" is allowed.

SURPRISE!

26

EXPECT
TO BE
SURPRISED.

Some people hate to be surprised. These folks map out a vacation like it was a strategic battle plan. To make the most of your fun time, these people say, you must plan, plan, plan so you don't waste a single minute getting lost, standing in long lines during the hottest part of the day, or wandering around looking at nothing when you could be staring at a very significant "Scenic Wonder of the World." They memorize maps of all kinds (road, amusement park, zoo) and never leave for a trip unprepared for any type of emergency (first aid kits, pain medication, and enough snacks to feed a small nation for a week). For them, half the fun of an excursion is preparing for it. The challenge *for them* is the ability to stay open to enjoying whatever comes up that didn't make it into their agenda for the day.

On the other hand, some other people are wide open for surprises. These are the people who are often seen lost, standing in long lines during the hottest part of the day, and wandering around looking at nothing. They're lousy map readers and are frequently in some sort of crisis requiring a Band-Aid. They are also hungry most of the time and dependent on the people who plan—those who have brought food. And if it weren't for them, the planners would probably never ever know the joy that the unexpected can bring.

Case in point: Ben and I love to hike in Virginia's mountains, and one of our favorite spots is Humpback Rocks in Shenandoah National Park. There's a short, steep trail there—about a 45-minute hike—that leads up to a spectacular view. We had walked it many times, so one day as we pulled up to the visitor center, I suggested that we take the long way up—about an hour and a half hike—because we'd never done that before. Ben, the cautious one, said, "I don't think that's a good idea. We're getting a late start, we don't have a detailed map of the area, we didn't bring backpacks, and since we've never done this trail before, we don't really know where we'll end up." But I, the impulsive one, said, "Oh, come on. The guy at the visitor center told us to just follow the signs. Besides, we need a little adventure in our lives!" So the cautious one sighed and capitulated against his better judgment, agreeing to take the new-to-us trail.

Thus, we walked...and walked. After an hour and a half, it appeared that we weren't going to find the sign that said "Humpback Rocks," so I admitted we should have stuck with the sure thing, and we turned around to hike back from whence we came. After about ten minutes, we started up an incline when I saw Ben, who was forging ahead of me, suddenly turn pale, back up, look at me and say, "Uh oh."

He motioned at me to stop, and I asked him what was wrong. "Bear!" he whispered, and I thought my heart would stop. We had never encountered a bear before, but we had read way too much about them to want to get a closer look. We knew that this one, if he wanted to, could outrun, outclimb, and outwhack us. So we turned around and quietly started walking the other way. But to where? We really didn't know exactly; we only knew we didn't want to cross his path again.

Fortunately, we ran into a group of four backpackers who had a map of the area and told us that, according to their map, if we went "thataway" down the Appalachian Trail, it would lead us to the visitor center parking lot in a mile. Overjoyed, I started singing and tripping merrily along downhill, chattering on about how good it felt to be in the home stretch of this fiasco (it was around 2:30, and we'd had no food or water or rest since breakfast). He responded by saying, "We aren't there yet." Such a cynic, I thought. Well, a mile downhill should have taken us about 30 minutes at the most, but we continued that trek for about an hour. He wanted to turn back after 30 minutes, but I just had a feeling we would come to the parking lot any second…until the trail wound around to the other side of the mountain and started going up! There was nothing to do but turn around and trudge uphill for another three hours, back to where we came from, back past the bear spot…back, back, back, up, up, up.

I must tell you that the cautious one, now also the man of steel in my book, amazed me in a couple of ways. He *never* wanted to stop and rest. I know that he was partially fueled by adrenaline, knowing we were running out of daylight and that if we didn't get out by dark, we'd have to spend the night in the woods with Mr. Bear and who knows what else. I *had* to rest periodically, but instead of giving me a hard time about my bad judgment, he was very sweet and encouraging. (I figured he was saving the verbal flogging for later.) He never mentioned the fact that if we had done what *he* wanted, we would have been sitting around a hotel pool about then, living the good life, and peeling grapes for each other.

As we were about to pass Mr. Bear's lair, he told me just to keep talking, because we needed to make noise so we wouldn't startle him if he were still around. So I kept announcing to bears at random, "Well, here come those nasty-tasting, bitter-fleshed, overfat hikers. Blechhhh. Who in the world would want a mouthful of that?" while Ben sang the chorus to "Yellow Submarine" more times than I could count.

Around 5:30, tired and hungry, we came to the backpackers' campsite, close to the parking lot where our car was. They had a cell phone, and when they saw us, one of them got on the phone and told somebody, "They're back. You can call off the search." The search? I immediately perked up. How exciting! We had never had a search party after us before! When the four backpackers had seen that our car, which we had described to them earlier, was still in the parking lot so late, they had called the park service to come looking for us. As it turned out, they found out that their map was outdated, and the Appalachian Trail had been rerouted, so they eventually knew they had sent us the wrong way. Had we kept going, we'd be in Georgia by now.

You may be asking yourself, where was the joy in *that* unexpected event? Are you kidding? Aside from being a time of concentrated prayer and fasting, this crisis made me see just how strong and patient my husband could be; we actually had a search party looking for us; and it made great material for our Christmas letter that year, not to mention a fine tale to tell our grandchildren someday.

Besides, God operates in surprise mode often—mostly notably in the birth of Jesus. Imagine being the aged Zechariah when an angel comes to him and says, *"Your wife Elizabeth will bear you a son,"* to which he, understandably surprised, says, *"How can I be sure of this? I am an old man and my wife is well along in years"* (Luke 1:13, 18).

Furthermore, imagine being Mary, a very young lady, when an angel (they often seem to be agents of the unexpected) says, *"You will be with child and give birth to a son,"* to which she, understandably surprised, says, *"How will this be,... since I am a virgin?"* (Luke 1:31, 34).

Just think of it! To birth the forerunner of the Savior of the world and the Savior of the world, Himself, God chose the most unlikely of women: a barren, menopausal woman and a young virgin!

In all of this life—in the life-changing moments and even in the light-hearted ones—it pays to be open to the pop quizzes God decides to spring on us once in a while. And even if the surprise isn't one we planned—even if it wasn't on our map—the path is much more adventurous when we embrace the unexpected and keep on hiking.

TRY THIS

Does the unexpected unnerve you? Then it's helpful to practice putting yourself in situations where there is no plan, no agenda, or where you are not in control of everything. Arrange for a fun activity with no agenda. Take a day trip with no schedule. Better yet, take a road trip with no destination! Okay, if that's too much, schedule a day with absolutely no plans. Or surprise someone else and unnerve them.

TURKEY BIRD

27

The *empty nest* (how I *hate* that term—as if the state of the home life God has given me in this season could actually be void of meaning and purpose) is a sign that life is changing, that my role will never be quite the same, that the nest doesn't really feel very safe any more.

Someone once said that this stage of life—when your kids have grown up, your parents have grown old, and even your own body has started showing signs of betrayal—is like waking up in your own house one morning realizing that someone has rearranged all the furniture. You recognize a lot of things, but they've all shifted. Some things are gone and a couple are new, but mostly everything just looks…different. It doesn't feel like home

BE UN-RESPONSIBLE.

any more, and you start to wonder if you'll ever feel the warmth of complete security again.

And it is often at this time of life that your role changes from being one of the younger ones to being one of the older, responsible ones. If this is happening to you, don't think you're all alone when you find yourself wanting to run away from the role and the responsibility. Let me guess: You don't want to be in charge of the holiday dinner; you want to sit at the kids' table. You don't want to feel responsible for everyone's good time at Christmas; you want to wake up, run down the stairs in your footed pajamas, and be dazzled by the magnificent surprises under the tree—surprises that appeared while you were sleeping. You don't want to think about mortgages and having enough money to put kids through college; you want to just live in the house, and then leave it to go to college yourself. You don't want role reversals, or worse, people who have been there for you your whole life to have the nerve to up and die on you; you just want to be the kid forever in a nice, safe place.

But, alas, you feel as though you must stop being the kid and start being an adult, so you do something rash like I did and try to cook Thanksgiving dinner.

Now I know that cooking a big meal is a snap for many women far younger than me; however, domesticity has never been one of my spiritual gifts. I have to work at it very hard, and even then, food just often turns out wrong. What's supposed to be hot ends up cold, what's supposed to be cold ends up warm, and what's supposed to be chewable ends up breaking dentures.

Well, for Thanksgiving, my biggest challenge was the turkey. You would think that after several Thanksgivings of fowl cookery, I would have turkey prep nailed, but it wasn't that easy for me. The first year, I didn't realize that it took *days* to thaw. How much sense does *that* make? Of course, then, it took way longer to cook than I had anticipated (so who was going to starve in a couple hours?), and when it was finally done, the formerly frozen insides yielded a surprise: that plastic bag full of what they call giblets—leftover "mystery" parts that get shoved back into the turkey when no one is looking.

Anyway, that year we all had a big laugh about Jill cooking the bag inside the bird. Ha-ha, wasn't that cute.

The next year, I was so much wiser: I bought the turkey a week ahead of time, thawed it, pulled out a plastic bag full of giblets, and stuck it in the oven. I was so very proud of myself...until it was done and Ben's brother, who was the designated carver, sliced into it, started laughing, and pulled out another bag—no kidding. This one had the neck in it. But honestly, I fished the directions out of the trash, and they distinctly said to remove the *bag* (singular) from the cavity. Ha-ha. We all had an even bigger laugh, since it was the second time we ate whatever toxins those plastic bags emitted within our turkey.

The third year, I was a woman on a mission. If we ate nothing else that Thanksgiving, we would eat a bagless turkey. So I bought the turkey in plenty of time, and when it thawed, we had a little talk. I laid it on the counter, with its little drumsticks facing me. As I stuck my hand in the cavity, it reminded me of my first visit to the gynecologist, and I suddenly felt compelled to apologize. "Is this your first time?" I asked it, compassionately. "I understand. Look, you may feel a little discomfort, but if you just relax, it'll be over with in just a couple of minutes." (Fortunately, I was alone in the kitchen at the time.) Then I searched the carcass for the bags. I found one, but couldn't seem to locate the other.

"Sorry, hon," I said as I then hoisted it into the air and shined a flashlight into the darkness. And to my delight, there sat the other bag, way in the back. Triumphantly, I fished that one out and stuck the turkey in the oven. That became my first bagless Thanksgiving dinner. We all cheered. I was proud, but couldn't help thinking, "This being responsible act is for the birds."

The good news is, you can be *un*-responsible (not to be confused with irresponsible) while you are being responsible... because God is the One who is ultimately responsible, and He can give us the freedom we need to celebrate life at its deepest and fullest, even in times of unsettling change.

There's something about having a close, intimate relationship with Him that puts us back where we belong—in the position of children. Though we still have to be in charge of a few things, it's like a parent saying to a child, "Okay, here's this job you need to do. I'll tell you how to do it every step of the way, and I'll be right here with you to help you." So we know that, since a higher, wiser One is in control, we can let go.

Jesus said, *"If you hold to my teaching, you are really my disciples. Then you will know the truth, and the truth will set you free"* (John 8:31–32). If you are mired in responsibility, I'm guessing you could use the freedom of this truth: God is in charge, not you.

Fortified with this reminder, I hope you find some un-responsible thing to do in the middle of all your duties. If it's Christmas, for instance, remember that from God's perspective, you *are* sitting at the kids' table, and you *are* free to find a few surprises He has for you that you yourself did not buy, wrap, or cook. Any time of year, remember you are free to do something a little—dare I say it?—impulsive, like I did one year.

We were at an open house at our minister's home. I was wearing my red suit and my tights with holly printed all over them. It was a good day. The kids were all outside, gathered around a vine that he was showing them—a vine that would allow you to hop on, swing across a wide ditch, and land safely on the other side. All the kids wanted to swing. I watched them from the window. It looked like so much fun. But I was a grown-up, and there were no other grown-ups out there. Plus, I was in a suit, with a skirt on....

But finally, I could resist the impulse no more. I walked outside, asked for a turn, hopped on the vine, swung across the ditch with amazing elegance, landed safely on the other side, and triumphantly walked back into the house, incredibly satisfied. I'm telling you, those few seconds of freedom put my grown-up life in perspective.

People had been looking out the window, wondering who that rather large red figure was, whooping across the ditch. "Oh," explained someone, "it's only Jill." Indeed—freed by God Himself to be un-responsible for a while.

TRY THIS *Are you tired of being "in charge" these days? I can't remove your responsibilities from your life, but I can suggest that you do something un-responsible every now and then. Children are good guides for this. At your next function, watch kids and do what they do for awhile. For instance, after dinner, are they obsessed with getting the kitchen cleaned? No; they just want to go out and play. Go out with them.*

GRAND CANYON

28

STOP
AND SIT
ALREADY!

I know; you're busy. But you absolutely must learn to sit down and be quiet for a little while.

I learned this lesson when Ben and I decided to spend our 25th wedding anniversary in the company of mules.

Since our first glimpse of the Grand Canyon years ago, we'd wanted to walk to the bottom and back out; the scenery was amazing, we enjoyed hiking and, as an added bonus, we knew the Grand Canyon was bear free (see "Surprise!"). We didn't especially want to make the trek alone, so we signed up for a mule-assisted backpacking trip. I had never heard of this before, but it brought to mind beasts of burden in little porter's hats, hooves outstretched at the trailhead, saying, "Take your bag, ma'am?" It turned out to be the best of both worlds. You could say you hiked the Grand Canyon, but actually carry only your essentials—water and gorp (trail mix made of peanuts, raisins, and never enough M&M's)—while the mules haul your camping gear, food, and clothes. Poor things. It was a great concept.

Excited, Ben and I started planning in earnest for this trip of a lifetime. We spent hours on the stair climber, huffing and puffing and sweating. We lifted weights and practiced walking with a loaded pack. We collected lists and talked with people who had been there, done that.

I might add that, at this point, my life was in a funky kind of transition. I was trying to adjust to the idea that our only child had left home for college, and face the fact that ever after she would probably come home only as a visitor. In addition, my moods were dipping and diving like a trick dolphin on heavy caffeine. It seemed as though everything in my life was changing, out of my control, like there was no safe place for me to land.

And then came September 11, 2001. Terrorists attacked the Pentagon in Washington DC and the World Trade Centers in New York City.

Now it wasn't just *my* world that lacked a safe place; it was *the* world.

Like many other people, I grieved and cried and prayed, asking God many questions. In the days that followed, when I woke up in the morning, it would be like every other morning for a split second...until I remembered. Then fear and distress crowded out the peace that I, as a "good Christian," was supposed to be feeling.

We were scheduled to leave September 22 for Arizona, which is a long way from Virginia. I fretted and stewed about flying, about being so far from Jamie during such an unsettled time. I was ready to take the cell phone on the plane and write Jamie a letter to leave behind, just in case. I asked a pilot friend

if *he* would fly at that time, I asked him if he would let his wife and kids fly at that time, and then I asked him a bunch of other questions, all in an attempt to gain some peace of mind about the whole trip. No peace of mind came, however, until I came upon some Scripture the day before we were to leave. I was reading about God's message to the Israelites through Isaiah:

> So *do not fear, for* I *am with you;*
> *do not be dismayed, for* I *am your God.*
> I *will strengthen you and help you;*
> I *will uphold you with my righteous right hand.*
> —Isaiah 41:10

Ohhhh…and that meant on a plane to Phoenix, too. I actually slept part of the way there.

Once we arrived at Grand Canyon National Park, we had an instruction session the day before we were to hit the trail, and we met the other people in our group, whom I had envisioned as being athletic mountain men, all in their twenties, all spending the last two years competing in Ironman triathlons. Imagine our surprise when the group gathered, and we were the *youngest* people there! Yes, half of the people in the group were in their fifties, the other half in their sixties. Several people were old enough to be my parents. We were amazed and relieved. At least we wouldn't be slowing anybody down on our way out of the canyon.

At this session, the instructor said, "Okay, everybody gets ONE duffel bag (way too small, in my opinion), and it can't weigh over 30 pounds" (believe me, they weigh them!). We had to display everything we thought we were going to burden the mules with, and then he started pointing at most of the essentials I had packed, saying, "You won't need that or that or that…." I was dismayed. How could I look my best without my stuff? Myra, an experienced backpacker in her sixties, told me not to worry—that she didn't even change underwear on a trip like this (three days, two nights). Whoa. I had my doubts about that one.

Anyway, at 6:15 the next morning, we gathered and began our descent into the canyon. It took about five hours and was actually very pleasant: beautiful scenery, plenty of water, gobs of gorp...what more could you ask for? Smugly, I congratulated myself for not being one of those wusses riding mules. Toward the end, I did notice a few blisters on my feet, and the temperature was noticeably warmer the closer we got to the bottom. In fact, when we were about 20 minutes from our campground, we made a big mistake: we looked at the thermometer. It registered 101 degrees! I immediately hit the wall. Oddly enough, Myra (again, who was way older than me, was from New Zealand, and had never experienced a temperature of 101 degrees in her life) seemed to be fine.

That evening, we pitched our tents, ate some more gorp, and marveled at the beauty of the canyon at sunset. Then, after a dinner of freeze-dried lasagna, prunes, and gorp, Ben and I had a romantic tryst in our tent, duct taping each other's feet, sweating (the temperature never got below 80 degrees), and popping ibuprofen like candy. "Ah, this is the life," we said. "Happy anniversary."

The second day we went on a three-hour hike ("to keep your muscles from getting stiff," said our guide. Ha! Too late). When we came back from that hike, we drank lemonade, ate some gorp, and, like dummies, checked the thermometer again. It showed 108! We smelled completely noxious but found a certain amount of freedom in that, because we didn't care about our unwashed hair or our unshaven body parts (legs or faces)...heck, I didn't even care about changing my underwear. Myra was right.

It was in this sickening heat of the afternoon, though, that we made a magnificent discovery that turned my spirit around: Bright Angel Creek. We had to cross the creek on our way back

to camp, and the most delicious feeling came over me as I stuck a hot foot into that cool, rushing water—so delicious that I wanted very much just to sit down right in the middle of it, even though I had all my clothes on.

So I did.

And I stayed there...for an hour.

And there, with my blisters and sore muscles in the middle of atmospheric conditions that rivaled hell, knowing I had the biggest physical challenge of my life ahead of me, I sat in the middle of beautiful, clear, cool water rushing all around me, with an electric blue sky above and the sun setting the canyon on fire in shades of red and gold. I sat there and talked to God about everything: about Jamie; about me getting older, her getting older, our changing roles, and my hormones running rampant all over my life; about September 11 and evil, grief, innocent lives lost, no safe place, and being terrified of terrorists; about how good it was to see Ben peeking at me through the bushes, making sure I was okay; about how this much beauty must certainly be a taste of what heaven is like.

An hour later, I came out of the water refreshed from the inside out.

At this point, I could describe the next day's hike out of the canyon for you. But I won't take the time to tell you about breaking camp at 3:30 A.M. to avoid the heat and hiking in the dark for a couple of hours; or about three hours into the ascent being ready to sell my camera, my water, and the M&M's out of my gorp for a ride on one of those mules with people (not provisions) on them; or about our guide urging us to keep eating, and that by the fourth hour, "gorp" sounded very much like a cross between "gak" and "urp" to me, and I never, *ever* wanted to eat another handful of that junk again; or even about emerging at the top—finally—applauding and congratulating each other.

No, I won't take time to tell you about all that, because the trip out isn't what I remember most. Ironically, as I've thought about it so many times since then, my highest moment came at the bottom of the canyon in Bright Angel Creek.

Even though, after my great time there, the blisters were still on my feet, the air was still awfully hot, and I still had that daunting climb ahead of me the next day, the time I took to sit in a creek changed the way I looked at everything, because God had given me the gift of re-creation—the same gift He offers us so often, and so often we decline. We're just too busy, you know, to go somewhere and *do nothing* for even a few minutes. And oddly enough, we're even less inclined to steal away for some quiet time when we need it most: during stressful, demanding days when our to-do lists are long and our energy reserves (emotional and physical) are dive-bombing toward empty.

But recall that even Jesus took the time to escape periodically, often after exhausting days of taking care of insatiably needy people. More than once, He left those needs unmet for a time so he could replenish His body and spirit alone with God. Mark describes one of those times when, *"Very early in the morning, while it was still dark, Jesus got up, left the house and went off to a solitary place, where he prayed"* (Mark 1:35). Of course, people (in this case, Simon and his companions) eventually found Him, as they had a habit of doing, whether Jesus escaped to the mountains or the lake. And, as you already know well, people and problems will eventually find you, too.

But you should escape anyway, and resist your inclination to tell yourself that "sitting in the creek" will take too long, your clothes will get wet, and besides, it won't change anything.

On the contrary, it will change *everything*, because God will change your perspective when you take time out to be in the moment. His moment.

When you get back to business, your pain will still be there; the heat—whatever pressure you were feeling before—will most likely surround you again, and the challenges you left will be waiting. But you will be different. You will be refreshed from the inside out—even at the bottom of your Grand Canyon.

TRY THIS

Are you in a low place right now—a place where there is pain or pressure, a place that doesn't feel comfortable or safe? Be sure to find some time every day—even if it's only for five minutes—to "sit in the creek," whatever that might be for you. What would bring you refreshment from the inside out? A glass of iced tea and five minutes of watching squirrels play in your yard? Writing in your journal? Lighting a candle and spending five minutes in prayer? You might want to plan even longer times to "sit in the creek"—a half day, a whole day, or a weekend if that's possible.

STORIES FROM

THE REST OF LIFE

ANNIVERSARY

29

HELP SOMEONE ELSE CELEBRATE!

Anyone who has spent 50 years on this earth married to the same person deserves more party than I could ever hope to throw. But when my in-laws, Arlene and Arthur, were approaching this big anniversary, Ben and I decided the least we could do was take a whack at it. We struggled for weeks trying to figure out a fun way to celebrate this occasion and, at the same time, give those who hadn't known them for 50 years a peek into their unparalleled relationship. Finally, we hit on an idea.

After we enjoyed a down-home dinner of roast beef, mashed potatoes, hot rolls, and that nostalgic dish from everybody's past that I refer to as "Jell-O with things in it," we met in the church sanctuary to take the "Arlene and Arthur Happy

Anniversary Quiz," illustrated with slides we had made from old photographs.

To set the scene, we had to tell the story about the interaction that characterized their relating pattern: On their wedding night, Arthur says that he gazed at his beautiful bride next to him, her hair shimmering in the moonlight, her face flushed in the afterglow of marital bliss, and whispered tenderly to her, "Sweetheart, would you like a glass of water?"

Lovingly she gazed back at him, touched by his thoughtfulness, and said, "Why yes, I believe I would."

"That's wonderful," he replied. "While you're up, will you get me one?"

And so it went…for the next 50 years.

The night of the party, with the help of the quiz, we celebrated one of the most unique relationships I have ever observed. For instance, we marveled at their amazing powers of communication:

> It's a typical evening. Arlene and Arthur are settled in, watching
> Wheel of Fortune on TV. Arthur grunts. That means he wants
>   A. to buy a vowel.
>   B. to change the channel.
>   C. to have Arlene make him some peanut butter crackers.

The correct answer is C. Arthur has eaten peanut butter crackers (made by Arlene) for lunch and at bedtime for more than 50 years. This would add up to well over 300,000—a mighty impressive number of crackers to make in a lifetime, if you ask me.

When I first visited the Baughan home, I was amazed that Arlene could distinguish Arthur's grunts like a mother can distinguish her child's cries. One evening at dinner, we were having butter beans. Arthur grunted. Arlene recognized the grunt to mean he wanted his butter beans in a separate dish. She also knows which grunt means, "I need some sweetener in my tea," and which grunt means, "Could you please butter my bread?" Fascinating.

I was really blown away one day when I was in the hall outside their bedroom, and I heard Arthur grunting rather pitifully. (It was frightening that after a few days, I, too, could distinguish one from another.) Afraid he had fallen and couldn't get up, I peeked in, only to find him lying on the bed with his bare feet stuck straight up in the air. "Are you okay?" I asked him, alarmed, thinking that either he had hurt himself or the gene pool I was about to marry into was deeply toxic. "Oh yes," he reassured me. "This is my 'sock grunt.' Arlene will recognize it and put my socks on me."

This is the honest truth.

Later he claimed he was doing it just to be funny. Riiiight.

The quiz also helped us celebrate Arthur's dependence on Arlene for other things as well:

Arthur is known far and wide for his
    A. *fashion sense.*
    B. *horse sense.*
    C. *nonsense.*

The answer could be any one of those, but we were looking for A. Wardrobe maintenance is definitely an issue in this relationship. Many times when Arthur dresses himself, his clothes, according to Arlene, aren't quite right: a few too many checks with plaids or a couple of colors that offend each other when worn on the same body at the same time.

One day, Arthur had had enough. Arlene had told him for the umpteenth time, "You're not going to wear that, are you?" He did the only thing he knew to do. Later, when Arlene realized she hadn't seen him for a while, she checked throughout the house and finally found him, all right—in the bedroom, sitting on the bed, defiantly unclothed, saying, "Okay, I'm not moving until you tell me what to put on."

And lest I'm making my father-in-law sound completely helpless, I must tell you that he is most definitely not. He has built three homes for his family, can wire all things electrical, spent 20 years helping to maintain our church building, has rescued me from a variety of catastrophes, such as locking myself out of my car and my house, and would do absolutely anything for his children and grandchildren.

So Ben and I were more than delighted to throw a party celebrating 50 years of marriage for two incomparable people. It was a lot of work, but during the months of preparations, I came across Proverbs 11:25, which reassures us that *"He who refreshes others will himself be refreshed."* Isn't that the truth! How often have you done something special for someone else with every intention of bringing good cheer to them, and in the end, you were the one who was most delighted? I will always look back on throwing this anniversary party as one of the greatest, most fun privileges of my life.

Arlene and Arthur claimed that they would never forget this celebration; that everything was just perfect, from the music to the entertainment to the Jell-O with things in it. But by about ten o'clock on the big evening, as the party was winding down, so were they, and we were hustling to get the happy couple out the door, because (Can you answer one more?):

> When Arthur travels, he wants to be
> A. *snorkeling in the Caribbean.*
> B. *riding camels in the Sahara Desert.*
> C. *home by dark.*

You guessed it.

TRY THIS

Is there someone you know who could use a celebration right now? Be the person to give them one they will never forget!

THE RULES

30

If the words "I really shouldn't be doing this at my age," have *ever* crossed your mind, I would love for you to join me in a manhunt for whoever made "the rules" about age-appropriate behavior.

I think we learned these rules when we were very young, watching other women in our families and communities and on TV. Here are a few I "caught":

REDEFINE WHAT IT MEANS TO BE "AT YOUR AGE."

The older you get, the funnier your shoes should look. I used to marvel at my grandmas' shoes—black lace ups with big thick heels. Those are what all the "older" women (older than what?) were expected to wear when I was a kid, and I always felt sorry for my grandmas, having to wear a style that had been around since the Revolution. They didn't seem to mind, though, so I figured that after a certain age, they took it for granted that they must start shopping at the old lady shoe store.

The older you get, the shorter your hair should be. Also, it must be curly. How many times have you heard (or just assumed) that after you get to be a certain age, you should cut your hair? In our neck of the woods, most ladies—but there are always rebels, of course—keep their hair cut short and permed and look askance at women who keep theirs long, unless the women are super old and wear it in a bun. My Grandma Ellis's weekly trip to Cleora's Beauty Shop in Liberty Center, Indiana, was a sacred, nonnegotiable time of hair washing, setting in rollers, sitting under the dryer…and, I suspect, catching up on the news around town.

The older you get, the more conservative your clothes should be. My grandmothers' dresses were generally dark or muted colors, below the knee, and always sleeved. Sometimes they had prints or polka dots, but that's about as wild as they got. Sometimes I try to picture my grandmothers in jeans and tank tops, and it just doesn't work in my mind. Must be the funny shoes.

The older you get, the more conservative your behavior must be. I don't remember any old ladies riding roller coasters at the street fair or running off to join the circus or starting new careers. Mostly they hung out on the farm and took enormous pride in what they could produce from the kitchen, which was, without a doubt, the best cuisine on earth. I wish I could talk to them now and find out if they ever dreamed of doing anything even slightly outrageous, like learning how to tap dance, but never did because they felt that it would not be socially acceptable.

The older you get, the less physically active you should be. I must say, I didn't learn this from my grandmothers, but from many people in general. The stereotype of the old person spending days on end in a rocking chair is close to the truth for some. Yes, I realize that we don't have the same bodies at 40, 50, or 60 that we had at 20, and I'm not advocating doing stupid things like sliding into home base when you've just been diagnosed with osteoporosis. But often I think we *expect* to get weaker and creakier, and it becomes a self-fulfilled prophecy more than an unavoidable destiny.

The older you get, the more comfortable you should be. When you get to a certain age, people tell you that you should think about retiring and doing *nothing*...or playing golf...or taking care of your own stuff—living life in maintenance mode and downsizing your world. This is what disturbs me the most about the rules.

Contrary to that thought pattern, Valerie Bell talks about having "soul goals" in life—goals that you can add to your list of temporal things to do before you die. One of the most magnificent soul goals she describes—one, in my view that can make life infinitely more exciting and fun and meaningful—is this:

> I want to remain open to the unexpected, off-the-beaten-path plans of God for my life. I intend to nurture an adventuresome spirit. Why not be open to things in my sixties that I would not consider at a younger age? Forget the small shockers like spitting and picking flowers from other people's gardens. I want to drape my soul in purple and be open to experiencing mission work in Kenya at sixty or a house filled with children at seventy. I want to develop an eagerness for the unconventional, path-less-traveled life. I am not motivated by the shock

appeal, however, but by the awareness that God can use
people whose boundaries with him are unconventional
and well off the beaten path.
—Valerie Bell, *She Can Laugh at the Days to Come*
(Grand Rapids; Zondervan, 1996)

I want to be one of those people who cross boundaries in every
area of life—in work and in play—don't you? I hope as I age that
people ask me with increasing frequency:

"Aren't you a little too old to be doing that?"

"When are you going to grow up?"

"Are you crazy?"

"What will people think?"

To which I will answer:

"No."

"Never."

"Yes."

"Who cares?"

I believe God would want it this way; it's often been His
standard method of operation in the past. Take Abraham and
Sarah, for instance. In their case, God messed with the boundaries of old age and showed that He could have a little fun with
them whenever He wanted.

Surely their circle of friends was abuzz when they found out
the couple was expecting a baby. Obviously, Abraham, at 100,
was—as Paul described him—a man of *"dead and shriveled loins"*
(Hebrews 11:12 *The Message*). (Fortunately for him, his legacy
didn't stop there.) Sarah, at 90, *"laughed to herself as she thought,
'After I am worn out and my master is old, will I now have this pleasure?'"*
(Genesis 18:12). Put yourself in her (probably funny) shoes.
I know my first reaction would be, "Do the *math*, Lord. I'll be 106
when this boy starts driving! What are you *thinking*?" And yet
God reminds them of His power in this plan when He asks, *"Is
anything too hard for the* LORD?" (Genesis 18:14).

Well, of course not—not in the life and times of Sarah and Abraham and not in the life and times of you and me. Consider yourself redefined...then go out and be ageless.

TRY THIS A *magnet on my refrigerator asks, "How old would you be if you didn't know how old you were?" Think about it. How old would you be? What might you do...or what would you like to do...if notions about being "your age" never entered your head?*

IT'S ALL RELATIVE

31

W hat do you know about your ancestors? Chances are, not enough.

Maybe, if your family is as fortunate as mine, there's someone in your bunch who has an obsessive desire to uncover and document your genealogy. My brother will travel anywhere for the opportunity to tramp around a cemetery looking for long lost relatives. The best part of his search results, though, is a book of photographs he put together for us, with pictures of our direct descendants as young children, young adults, and older adults. The first picture is of our immediate family (Mom, Daddy, Ted, and me) looking like the Cleavers, very clean and

TELL
STORIES.

very white. And each page thereafter takes you a little further back in time, where the clothes get weird and the names get weirder with each preceding generation. (My favorite is Angus; it sounds like such a take-charge and beefy name. However, for the life of me, I cannot imagine being the mother who looks into the sweet face of a newborn, turns to her husband, and says, "Oh honey...he looks just like an Angus. We must call him that.")

One day a few years ago, I was paging through the book and found myself longing to really know the people in it. Of course, I was acquainted with my own parents, but even my grandparents I knew only as sweet old people who loved their grandchildren and wanted to feed them all the time—not as real people with struggles and triumphs. And the rest of the relatives in the book, I'd never locked eyes with, not even once. I looked at the pictures and wanted to jump into them—catapult myself back in time to the day the picture was taken. I wanted to know the good, the bad, and the ugly about all of them, but all I had was an image of who they were. Only one had left a diary, and it was very sparse; there were a few letters, but that was about it. I however, wanted more: I wanted their stories.

And I found a way to get them.

One summer, when I was visiting home, I invited my mother's two sisters to come over; another afternoon, I invited my father's three sisters over; and on each of these occasions, we gathered at my mom's dining room table, where I had the photo album ready and waiting. I started with the oldest picture and said, "Okay, tell me everything you know about or heard about this person." Then I turned on the tape recorder and let them roll. It was magnificent. They told stories all afternoon, most of which I had never heard before, and I got it all on tape. The only person no one knew anything about was the gentleman in the oldest picture in the book. He was pretty rumpled and looked like he might have fallen off of his branch of the family tree a few times, so we can only imagine what he was like. But by the end of these two sessions, I finally felt as though I had a sense of the real people who came before me: the saints, the swindlers, the stoics, the party people, the salt of the earth, and the emotionally unstable. I knew that I loved them all, even if I didn't know them.

Someday I will transcribe these tapes and write personality portraits to accompany the photo album. Until then I'll treasure the taped memories. Since those two gab sessions, five of those precious family members have died; the stories might have died with them had we not spent those summer afternoons celebrating our family's story.

I intend to keep the stories coming, because if I don't, how will posterity know about the endearing habit my Grandma Ellis had? After visits from us grandchildren, she would for days refuse to clean our fingerprints off her windows, just so she could look at them and be reminded of us. And how will anyone ever know about my Grandma Pinney, who kept working in her garden so late in life that my uncle had to take the spark plugs out of her rototiller to keep her from running over herself? And how will anyone else know about the time when we paid a visit to my Uncle Tub and Aunt Bea, both in their eighties, who answered the door half dressed—he in his undershirt, she in her slip? Ben asked, "So, Uncle Tub, what have you been doing today?" to which Tub replied, "You'd be horrified if you knew what we'd been doing." Yikes. Never mind.

And what about…

Oh, I could go on and on. Chances are, so could you; and for that reason, I urge you to have some fun gathering these stories—not only for future generations, but for your own and your family's enjoyment now.

And if your family is so full of dysfunction that there are few stories you'd want to tell, or if you were adopted and don't really know anything about your ancestors, then remember this:

you need to tell your own story. Everybody has one—a life story made up of hundreds of tales. Tell them. Tell them all in some tangible way, on tape, on paper, on video.

I'm inclined to write things down and have kept a prayer journal for the past 12 years. I've told my daughter, Jamie, that when I die, she will read my prayers to God and find out what a mess I really am. As I read entry after entry of times I poured my heart out to God, year after year, I am struck by two things: my powerlessness to do this life well on my own and His faithfulness to stick with me.

I have plenty of company, it turns out, as documented by the psalmist when he recounts the history of the Jewish nation. Like me, they had a tendency to make the same mistakes over and over again. *"How often they rebelled against him in the desert and grieved him in the wasteland! Again and again they put God to the test"* (Psalm 78:40–41). I am dismayed to read pages of my prayers and find that I am still struggling with some of the same issues I struggled with ten years ago. You would think that by the time a person got to this point in life, said person would have her act together. Nay.

But if you look at my Bible, you can see hope. Often, when God would answer a prayer or give me some specific guidance or encouragement, I would write the date next to the passage. After years of doing this, I realized that I had created a kind of odd cross-referencing system. As a result, you can look at the date next to a passage and check the same date in my prayer journal to see what I was feeling or asking at the time; what struggles I was having and God's response to those struggles; what fun I was having and God's affirmation of that joy; what questions I was asking and God's answers.

One morning several years ago, I was having a bad time, feeling dead and dry; this "getting older" thing was getting me down, and I was feeling zero enthusiasm for anything on earth; all I could feel was emptiness and loss. I wrote in my journal:

"Oh Lord, I guess You've got me where You want me now. You brought me to this desert, lower than a snake's belly, drier than sand...please, just show me how amazing You are when You rain on the desert of my sadness...."

Minutes later, in my study for that morning, I heard from the Lord through these passages:

"I *will send rain.*"
—1 Kings 18:1

"I *will make rivers flow on barren heights,*
    and springs within the valleys.
I *will turn the desert into pools of water,*
    and the parched ground into springs....
so that people may see and know,
    may consider and understand,
that the hand of the LORD *has done this.*"
—Isaiah 41:18, 20

Time after time, story after story, God has written out His love for me, pulled me out of the pits, sat and cried with me, laughed with me, and laughed at me. I have wrestled with Him, asked Him angry questions, and sat in frustrated silence before Him. The dates in my Bible and the corresponding prayers in my journal write the story of my journey with Him. I want my descendants and anyone else to be able to look at my life story and see that no matter how many times you mess up, no matter how mad you get at Him, God will be around, waiting for a relationship with you, still in the business of working wonders in a life that can't always seem to get it together.

Share your stories for fun, yes, but even more importantly, as a testament to God's faithfulness in your life. Do as the psalmist did when he recounted the history of the Jewish nation, and vowed:

We will tell the next generation
the praiseworthy deeds of the LORD,
   his power, and the wonders he has done....
so the next generation would know them,
   even the children yet to be born,
   and they in turn would tell their children.
Then they would put their trust in God
   and would not forget his deeds
   but would keep his commands.
—Psalm 78:4, 6–7

Pass on family memories, and recount your own history for someone who needs to hear about God faithfulness.

TRY THIS

So what's your story? Better yet, what are your stories? Describe them into a tape recorder or video camera, or write them down—anything to share them with others. Is it time for you to do what I did and get some relatives together for a story swap?

The Attitudes

32

W e're all looking for mentors, no matter what age we are—people who have traveled difficult roads we've yet to start; people who have struggled through treacherous territory with unwavering courage; people who show us that it's possible to live through loss and emerge, thriving, on the other side of adversity. But is that what I'm looking for today?

Nah.

Right now I just want a mentor who can be nice and superficial and show me how to have some fun—fun that's not limited to bingo. Although bingo can be quite lively and even rowdy with the right crowd on a Friday night.

FIND A MENTOR.

A *good time mentor* is one who—no matter how old—somehow has a handle on the principles in this book. And while I'd love to be as physically fit as the man who recently celebrated his 88th birthday by making his 300th climb up McAfee Knob on Catawba Mountain in Virginia, a good time mentor is more for helping me develop or maintain an *attitude* of fun, not for helping me get in great physical shape.

Granted, finding a person who lives as if they are celebrating one wild party after another is difficult. Therefore I'm suggesting that we be on the lookout for women with maybe just one of the attitudes we're looking for—get to know them, take them to lunch, ask them how they got so good at this fun thing.

Surely you can think of a few of these people right now. I can: my friend Nanny, for example.

Nanny's son-in-law was throwing a surprise birthday party for her daughter. Nanny actually called me up one day and said, "Ted's throwing a 50th birthday party for Susan, and he's getting kind of cocky about it, since he's only 49. I'd like to surprise *him* by giving him a hard time. Can you do something stupid?" (Why do people call me whenever they want something stupid done?) Of course, I gathered a posse of crazies around, and we delivered. What made it so special, though, was the fact that it was Nanny's idea; she definitely had the attitude of mischief.

Or consider Ben's aunts, Edith and Marion, who were most excellent porch sitters. When they were out, it was impossible not to stop, even if only for a few minutes, and hang around with them. They were masters of the attitude of "stop and sit already."

And so many women of the generation before us were fabulous cooks who had a symbiotic relationship with food. Ben's grandmother, "Mamar," used to ask us over for lunch on Saturdays sometimes. Now to me, lunch on Saturday is grilled cheese and a can of soup; to her it was enough food to sink a ship. And after we had all loosened the waistbands on our britches and waddled away from the table in a mashed potato-induced stupor, she would exclaim in dismay, "Nobody has eaten a thing!" Obviously an untruth, but that lady takes the prize for the attitude of "fun with food in the kitchen."

And how about when my friend Delane came to church one day, sparkling up a storm. Looking closer, I discovered that she had glittered her skin just for fun. It made me want to run home and immediately glitter my own—most certainly the attitude of redefining what it means to be your age in action.

And then there's Eloise, a beautiful mother of three and grandmother of four, who never really retired from her job at the International Mission Board in Richmond, Virginia. I first encountered her at my church—not in person, but on a video screen. She was wearing a basketball jersey and a baseball hat on backwards, tossing a basketball in her hands. Taking note of her white hair and sweet face, we expected her to offer up milk and cookies; instead, the first words out of her mouth were, "What up, dawg?"

Huh? Everybody did a double take.

She continued:

We've got a situation, so I've got a challenge. Missionaries goin' overseas is wayyy up! But the Benjamins ain't comin' in! No mo'? No go! So here's the skinny: We need more Bennies!

So if I stuff the rock in the hole, you cough up the dough; If I put the biscuit in the basket, you put the scrilla in the plate! If I put the pill in the box, you put the cheddar in the bag....

Capiche?"

Immediately I wanted to *be* this lady.

Then she swung into action: "Get your transcripts out, homies! School's in session!"

And Eloise was off slam-dunking baskets and doing all manner of fancy footwork on the floor. Of course she wasn't really shooting hoops; she was slam-dunking from a lift they were using to get her up to the basket. But the fact that she was willing to ride up in the thing and pretend to slam-dunk basketball after basketball was enough to impress me.

And that's not her only performance; other videos she's done for the IMB have required her to walk across the table in the executive dining room, get into a kayak in the middle of the James River, be strapped into parasailing gear, then pretend to jump off Jockey's Ridge, a giant pile of sand dunes in North Carolina.

They chose her—and she accepted the challenges—not for her superior athletic ability, but for her willingness to embrace the attitude of trying something new. It has opened new doors for her, introduced her to new people—she's even signing autographs, for Pete's sake. At a time in life when it's easy to let your world shrink, hers has opened wide up.

I took her to lunch one day, and asked what her secret was—the source of her spirit of playfulness, despite a life that left her widowed twice and had its share of challenges. Her answer probably won't surprise you: "The Lord," she said, "has always been my hope and my strength."

Not unlike Naomi in the book of Ruth—Naomi who had also been widowed, and, in addition, left childless. She experienced depression, so much that she asked to be called Mara, which means "bitter." Still, she carried on with faith in God, thinking of her daughters-in-law before herself, urging them to go back to their people to start a new life. Orpah went. Ruth chose to stay with her, however, and together they coauthored with God the rest of His story for them. Ruth looked out for Naomi, and Naomi encouraged Ruth to seek out a relationship with the man who later became her husband, Boaz. The result: God's perfect plan, for Boaz and Ruth married and had a child, making Naomi a grandmother and prompting the women of the community to say, "Praise be to the LORD.... He will renew your life and sustain you in your old age" (Ruth 4:14–15).

Without a doubt, Naomi had the attitude of believing in renewal.

Isn't that what we all want? To be not only consistently sustained but also renewed? To reach that point where we have hope for the future and joy for the day? We can thank God for all kinds of women available to mentor us in these attitudes and to point the way to the party!

TRY THIS Start a search for older women who have a knack for finding the fun in any situation in life. Each time you find one with a great attitude of one kind or another, make an effort to get to know her. Take her to lunch; invite her into your life.

WHY WAIT?

33

CELEBRATE YOUR LIFE NOW.

For the past couple years, I have noticed a disturbing trend in even the most playful of people: we are quintessential *celebration waiters*, forever waiting till life's "big moments" to celebrate in a big way. We wait until golden or silver anniversaries, until big accomplishments or promotions until announcements that people are moving away, until birthdays that end in a zero.

Some of my favorite moments, however, have been spent celebrating *non*accomplishments. For instance, I have mentioned that my husband has spent much of his life immersed in being a Virginia Tech fan. That's fan as in "fanatic." He has season tickets to all the home games (and has gone in wind, rain, snow, sleet, and hurricanes), and keeps his game bag packed all year with rain gear, radio ears, pennants, magnets, whistles, and who knows what else.

For all this loyal devotion, I thought he deserved a little winging. So one Saturday in one November while he was at a game Tech was supposed to win, I painted our bathroom in big, 15-inch horizontal stripes of maroon and orange, Tech's colors. (The maroon was a nice conservative shade. The orange, however, I would describe as "electric Cheez Doodle"; it glows, in a cool, radioactive kind of way.) Then I put a Tech wallpaper border around the middle and some Tech paraphernalia up on the walls, and waited for him to come home, so we could celebrate the victory in grand style.

Well, when he arrived, he informed me that Tech had lost. When I showed him the bathroom, he loved it and we celebrated anyway. It is the tackiest room in the house, but, as you know, we are tacky people. It fits.

In the same vein, I knew a professor at a local college who threw an "I Didn't Get Tenure *Again*" party. Not getting tenure was still disappointing, of course, but having his friends around him eased the pain.

On a more positive note, I have friends who are not above celebrating weird stuff like the day *after* New Year's, the first fly (or other insect of your choice) of spring, getting over the flu, and finally potty training a three-year-old.

None of these occasions, however, can come close to being as offbeat as the gathering that honored a precious woman named Carolyn: she had the unparalleled opportunity to party at her own funeral before she died. As her pastor, James Lamkin, put it, "We knew Carolyn was dying. And we knew it would be sooner, rather than later. We knew our grief would be immense. We knew buckets couldn't hold our tears. We knew the strongest of stiff upper lips would sag under our loss. What to do? What should we do? How do you maintain bright hope *while facing* grim reality?"

Then someone came up with a great idea: to have a party for Carolyn that would celebrate the life and ministry of a woman who loved life. So they celebrated with full force. They had to get her permission, of course, and her first response was, "I don't know…it just sounds strange."

No kidding. Being invited to your own funeral is not the norm in these parts. Still, when Reverend Lamkin told her that she would be giving her church and community a great gift by being able to celebrate *with* them, she gave her permission.

Her friends booked a band: a "six-piece, bow-tied, bright-vested, straw-hatted Dixieland band." They brought food, and filled the tables with fried chicken, pies, and cakes (unmistakably Baptist); they formed a receiving line that gave each person a chance to hug Carolyn and speak to her.

Reverend Lamkin says:

I watched in grateful amazement. Honored was I, simply to be there. Just to be a witness. But amazement always sits second fiddle to awe. For as I stood in awed silence, her husband, her dear, dear husband [Walt]—whom she often referred to as a true prince, a real jewel—strolled softly across the patio. With his hand extended, Walt gracefully lifted her quietly waiting hand; the same hand he first held when she was 18 years old. Fifty-four years ago! And Carolyn, though dog tired, gently rose and found the strength to dance.

And dance, they did! Synchronized feet moving as one. Swinging in the sunlight.

But believe it or not, that's not all. Maybe it was accidental or providential? Or maybe Walt tipped the conductor—I don't know. But the band began playing "Just a Closer Walk with Thee."

No.

They didn't just play it. They performed it to the slow, sauntering rhythm of New Orleans jazz. I'm not sure if time collapsed or expanded. But I'm reasonably certain that linear time stopped, and vertical, eternal time began. Grace made space and time parenthetical.... It was an out-of-time, beyond time, moment. A moment Kodak couldn't capture. Waltzing Walt led. Dancing Carolyn followed. And friends and family and faith community applauded.

—James Lamkin, "The Last Dance" (Originally published on December 16, 1996, in the newsletter of the Ravensworth Baptist Church, Annandale, Virginia)

I have a feeling that all of heaven was applauding right along with them.

When Carolyn died, do you think there was a single person who regretted being a part of this celebration of her life? I can't believe so. And neither can I believe that we will regret commandeering every opportunity to celebrate this life while we are still living.

Even the psalmist urges us to see how *"This is the very day God acted—let's celebrate and be festive!"* (Psalm 118:24 *The Message*). And really, every day is the day God acts. So why not celebrate a thirty-*second* anniversary? A party to commemorate everyone who is *not* jumping ship in your life? (These are especially effective when you've had a series of friends who have moved away.) A party for a sixty-*fourth* birthday? Or better yet, a sixty-fourth and *a half* birthday?

Celebrating odd things at odd times can be a life-affirming, joy-producing exercise in itself—one that reminds us that God is all over our lives, and that every occasion deserves to be a special one.

TRY THIS

What are you waiting to celebrate? Go ahead, pull out all the stops (or keep it simple and small), and have a ball reveling in something that's on your plate now.

See You Later

34

My friend Debbie works for a cemetery, helping people preplan for the time when the family will be "picking up the pieces at the time of loss." I have complained to her about how somber the brochures and commercials are for this activity. Surely, I have thought, planning for your "final needs"—at least for the service itself—can be more fun than these people let on. And thus, inspired by Carolyn (see "Why Wait?"), I began my own "fun-eral" file: a collection of ideas for my own final earthly celebration. I'm doing this for a number of reasons, but mainly because I don't trust others to do the planning. People are typically not at their most

START A "FUN-ERAL" FILE.

creative when they are under emotional duress, not to mention a pressing time constraint. Plus, I figure that I can actually have a swell time collecting random ideas—a lot more fun than my family would have, trying to do it all in two days.

Furthermore, I have been in the little room with the minister, the family, and maybe a few friends, and asked to describe the deceased. This in itself can be problematic, because no one is completely good, yet that's what we tend to want to focus on during the funeral. For people who were real stinkers in this life, it may be difficult to come up with enough acceptable material for an entire service. So if you are one of these stinkers, you may want to start a file like mine and get your own service in order before someone else has a chance to mess it up.

You may think this sounds morbid, but think about it: People design the house of their dreams and the wedding of their dreams. Women search for the man of their dreams. Why not plan the fun-eral of your dreams?

Here are some random ideas from my file:

Select a theme. I think it should have a theme. I love what Anne Lamott says in her book, *Plan B: Further Thoughts on Faith*:

> I have grown old enough to develop radical acceptance. I insist on the right to swim in warm water at every opportunity, no matter how I look, no matter how young and gorgeous the other people on the beach are. I don't think that if I live to be eighty, I'm going to wish I'd spent more hours in the gym or kept my house a lot cleaner. I'm going to wish I had swum more unashamedly, made more mistakes, spaced out more, rested. *On the day I die, I want to have had dessert.* (Italics added)

This sentence of hers contains an idea I would like to adopt for my theme: "Maybe I'm in my dessert days, the most delicious course." That would be a great theme for a fun-eral: dessert. In keeping with this theme, I'd like to have banners that say things like "Dessert: It's What's for Dinner!" And favors should be given out—maybe refrigerator magnets that say, "Got dessert?"

List positive attributes. I made some notes about the positive points of my life and personality for which I'd like to be remembered. For instance, I wrote down that I'd like to be known as fearless, adventuresome, bold, and joyful. I'd like people to say: "She didn't waste a single day in self-pity or envy; she never skipped a daily quiet time with God and certainly never fell asleep on Him while she was praying early in the morning; she bounded out of bed at sunrise, eager to meet a new day, and never snapped at her early-bird husband, who delighted in waking her up by machine-gunning questions at her, such as, 'Hey, Jill! What's the capital of Minnesota? Hey, Jill! Can you spell Saskatchewan? Hey, Jill! What's on your calendar for the next two years?'" I listed as many of these attributes as came to mind.

Share the whole truth. I was very disappointed after I made this list, because my life doesn't really measure up to the eulogy I designed for myself. I myself have always wanted to go to a funeral where they told the whole truth, not just the good stuff, so I added the rest of the truth. And the not-so-comfortable truth I added is that for a significant portion of my life, I've been resistant to change, moody, lazy, and obsessive. As I wrote that down, I found the activity to be therapeutic. I then scripted out an interesting combination of all my characteristics so that whoever reads the eulogy can get through the good parts without laughing.

Identify favorite Scriptures. Some of my favorite Scriptures also went in the file, such as, *"You're here to be light, bringing out the God-colors in the world.... Shine! Keep open house; be generous with your lives. By opening up to others, you'll prompt people to open up with God"*

(Matthew 5:14, 16 *The Message*). I want the Scriptures to remind everyone present that even though I've gone on ahead, they are still here and need to be carrying on with gusto.

Know that these plans will probably change over time because, as my pastor is fond of saying, "You live your funeral every day." So have fun adding touches as life goes on; your fun-eral file will only get richer as you live this imperfect life.

As a result of starting my fun-eral file, I've taken a long, hard look at the What I Hope People Will Say About Me list, and I've found it's a good list to revisit from time to time when I lose perspective and forget that this life is only the beginning, no matter how old I am.

Some day when I'm...oh, who knows how old...at my fun-eral, I hope someone will stand up and say something like this:

> Jill Baughan—yes, we all know she was far from perfect.
>
> She struggled with her weight, beginning with kindergarten, when she was known as Big Truck. She was known to shift from left to right on Weight Watchers weigh-in day to get the lowest possible number on the scale. She had an obsessive affection for chocolate— she lived for dessert.
>
> People were always telling her "you think too much," calling her The Ruminator, and comparing her to a cow that chewed its cud, swallowed it, urped it back up, and chewed some more. "Move on to the next thought/task/ obsession already," they would say.
>
> Rather an exhibitionist, she loved the sound of her own voice in a microphone, and people got really tired of hearing her attempt to sing "Danke Schoen" whenever she got her hands on one. She could not sing.
>
> She hated getting up in the morning, was lazy, really, and was an expert at goofing off. She searched every

translation of the Bible to find goofing off as a spiritual gift...with no luck. She disliked most cooking, killed most house plants, and procrastinated on most house cleaning. She drove her husband crazy by being so scatterbrained, forgetting stuff all the time. She had a hard time with midlife, envying people who could have all the children they wanted, struggling with turning loose the one she had. She was always, she complained, missing someone somewhere for so much of her life. She was tired of missing people. And she had such a fear of failure and lack of faith that when God assigned her to author a book about having fun, it took her 16 years to get around to writing it.

But in spite of all this, He used her anyway, as God is prone to do with all of us, in spite of our truths. And that is why we are celebrating today. That's why there are balloons tied to the pews and party poppers in every seat. That's why you were asked not to wear black as a sign of mourning, but to wear it only if it makes you more celebrative because you feel it makes your hips look thinner. That's why there are huge baskets of Reese's peanut butter cups at the doors. Please take as many as you want when you exit; there are enough for 125 per person. That's why the celebration will move from this worship center at Cool Spring Baptist Church out into the sunshine of this beautiful day, where we can enjoy a fantastic meal of carbohydrates and desserts. For those of you who must have meat, we have a special treat: turkey without a single plastic bag cooked inside and freshly tweezed ham hocks.

And that's why, after we have feasted and talked and laughed to our hearts' content, the celebration will last until evening, when we will all dance under the stars, and even nondancers will shake a leg, unafraid of looking stupid. Original hits by the original artists will be the order of the evening, featuring some of Jill's favorites: the Monkees singing "I'm a Believer," the Beatles' rendition of "Twist and Shout," Aretha Franklin belting out "Respect," Earth, Wind & Fire singing "September," Kurt Carr's version of "In the Sanctuary," Robin Mark's "Days of Elijah," Steppenwolf's "Born to Be Wild" (of course), Mary Mary's "Shackles," and "Under the Sea," sung by that lobster from The Little Mermaid. Also, we will gallop our pretend horses to the tune of the "William Tell Overture" performed by the Richmond Symphony. And finally, everyone will sing along as the Brooklyn Tabernacle Choir performs their most spectacular rendition of the "Hallelujah Chorus," because—Hallelujah, praise God, and thank You, Jesus—Jill Baughan is in heaven and is having the time of her life!

As you leave tonight, go in peace, go in joy, check out the fireworks in the parking lot…and feel free to take some dessert home with you. There's plenty.

TRY THIS

Okay, all it takes is a file folder. Toss in ideas, even if they're only on random bits of paper. Include songs, descriptions, people, and whatever else you want. And if you like, you can throw in some ideas about what you don't want. Think this way: If there were no limits (such as time, space, or money), what kind of fun-eral would you have? What does this description tell you about your life so far? What does it tell you about how you want to live the rest of your life?

HEAVEN

35

M aybe you're not one to dwell a lot on what heaven will be like, because it's so hard to imagine. Eternity? Beyond the scope of our imagination, for sure. But I have discovered that I love thinking about heaven in a way that gives me hope, a way that makes me focus on life, not death, and reminds me that my motor isn't really winding down; as a matter of fact, it's just revving up.

I love thinking about heaven in the light of exhilaration and joy....

For instance, I believe that heaven will be full of the kind of fun you had as a kid: carefree, with lots of laughter. We will be new creations in Christ, with the

IT'S LIKE THIS...

best of childhood and the best of adulthood in us. He will show us how to view life with a new perspective—His—and maybe we'll even be able to eat fried things and immediately ride the Tilt-A-Whirl without getting sick.

Heaven will be the ultimate second chance. For all the delightful opportunities that we so obtusely passed up at one time or another, we will experience the ultimate faithfulness of God—one more chance, but this one's a doozy: it lasts forever.

In heaven, we will be secure in our identity, and it will never include the word "big" used in a derogatory way. We will enjoy being completely known, inside and out, by God, who will give us a name that captures the essence of who He made us to be.

In heaven, we will experience the most fun and comforting kind of community imaginable, knowing that we will never have to do life alone.

In heaven, we will be released from our past dumb mistakes and able to enjoy the complete freedom that comes with complete forgiveness.

Heaven, I believe, will be a place of activity rather than passivity, where we are continually searching for and finding our joy.

In heaven, we will remember—and smile.

And furthermore…

In heaven, there will be no fear that we must push aside; we will be all about courage and adventure.

I would hope that there would be toilet paper in heaven; however, I cannot personally guarantee this. Suffice it to say that there will be plenty of lively ways for us to express our affection for each other, and everything will indeed be beautiful in its time.

In heaven, we will all be naked with candy…so to speak. Inhibitions will go flying out the window as we celebrate God all day every day.

In heaven, we will not be continually longing for some big event to take place, because we will be living the biggest event ever…and enjoying every moment of it.

In heaven, we will not have to ask boys out ever again, I pray. God will be busy, though, amazing us with stories about how many times He was able to do more for us than we ever imagined, even in our play.

Will there be animals in heaven? Who knows? Either way, I am certain that God will give us many opportunities to connect with His creation. I hope at least part of heaven smells like a barn.

And if there's anything that resembles a Reese's peanut butter cup in heaven, we should start thanking God right now.

Even better…

In heaven, we will have perfect, new bodies, and we won't hesitate to accept invitations to hot tubs.

In heaven, we will have no trouble "thinking outside the wineskin," whether it comes to work or play.

In heaven, we will all, without a doubt, know what we were made to do—and we'll actually be doing it!

Heaven, I am convinced, will be the best party anyone ever threw.

There will never be a shortage of wonder in heaven; it will be saturated with awe and mystery and the excitement of discovery.

Please, God, tell me there will be chimpanzees in heaven. And if there aren't, I know that, even without primates, we won't miss a single fleeting opportunity for joy there.

In heaven, we will never feel the need to escape to a vacation, because our everyday life will be better than the most exotic destination we could ever dream up.

And how about this…

In heaven, joy and sorrow will not need to walk hand in hand, because there will be no sorrow.

In heaven, I believe, we will be continually sharing one another's gifts and passions. And football will finally make sense to me.

Our faith will be perfect, so there will be no fear of trying anything new.

Our dreams will be realized at last, and we will be able to soar like eagles, and "ride the heights of the land."

I believe heaven will be full of the anticipation of God's surprises.

We will enjoy being un-responsible, relaxing in God's capable hands, all of us sitting at the biggest kids' table imaginable. God Himself will cook the turkey.

In heaven, every place will be a safe place, and there will be a creek full of refreshment whenever and wherever we need one.

And best of all...

In heaven, there will be endless opportunities to help one another celebrate.

In heaven, we will break every rule about getting older, because we won't be getting older. I wouldn't be surprised to see my grandmas' funny shoes there, however.

We will tell story after story, smiling and laughing and knowing that the Author of each of our stories was just beginning to write them during our time on earth.

We will meet up with the people who arrived in heaven before us, and we will have a chance to thank them for showing us how to squeeze the gladness out of life—even when life on earth wasn't so glad.

We will often look for ways to celebrate the smallest and the goofiest of occasions.

And we will laugh when we think about our fun-erals, slapping each other on the back, wondering why we didn't celebrate with even more noise, more music, more balloons, more party poppers, and more sugar.

At least that's how I think it will be: sheer joy. And since you may not be making the trip this afternoon, it's important to remember that on your best days and even on your worst days, heaven—at least a taste of it—starts now if only you'll accept God's invitation to tap into your passionately eager, enthusiastically wild self, and rediscover one of His most exquisite gifts: the freedom of fun.

TRY THIS

Do you believe that you can have a little taste of heaven on earth? What can you do to make sure you stay in touch with that vision and the way it's manifested right where you live? Take a few moments to write your own personalized description of heaven. Then—knowing your future is not only secure but also full of celebration—go out and do as Paul suggests:

> *Live a lover's life, circumspect and exemplary, a life Jesus will be proud of: bountiful in fruits from the soul, making Jesus Christ attractive to all, getting everyone involved in the glory and praise of God.*
> —Philippians 1:10–11 (*The Message*)

New Hope® Publishers is a division of WMU®,
an international organization
that challenges Christian believers to understand
and be radically involved in God's mission.
For more information about WMU, go to www.wmu.com.
More information about New Hope books
may be found at www.newhopepublishers.com.
New Hope books may be purchased at your local bookstore.

Other Books you may enjoy

Good for Goodness' Sake
*7 Values for Cultivating Authentic
Character in Midlife*
Gary Fenton
ISBN 1-59669-009-7

**When the Glass Slipper
Doesn't Fit**
Claire Cloninger and Karla Worley
ISBN 1-56309-437-1

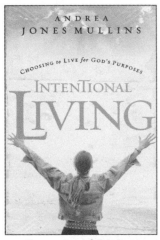

Intentional Living
Choosing to Live for God's Purposes
Andrea Jones Mullins
ISBN 1-56309-927-6

Available in bookstores
everywhere

For information about these books
or any New Hope products, visit
www.newhopepublishers.com.